CAMBRIDGE
Global English

for Cambridge Primary English as a Second Language

Learner's Book 5

Jane Boylan & Claire Medwell

Series Editor: Kathryn Harper

Contents

Contents

Contents

	Writing/Projects	Use of English	Cross-curricular links	21st-century skills
	Guided writing: Write a newspaper report Write about an ancient building Break a hieroglyphic code	Subordinate clauses Imperative forms Prepositions of time, location and direction	**History:** Egyptian inventions	**Values:** Being selfless **Critical thinking:** Make personal opinions about ancient civilisations
	Guided writing: Write a descriptive text about a rainforest animal Made a 3D model of a rainforest Raise money to help protect rainforests	Present perfect Adverbs of degree Adjective order	**Environment:** Protecting our planet	How can we protect our rainforests **Values:** Protecting animal habitats **Critical thinking:** Share opinions on life in the rainforest and the dangers it faces
	Guided writing: Design and write a leaflet Do a nature study Made a poster	Personal pronoun it/its Gerunds and infinitives Compound nouns	**Science:** Animal camouflage	Understanding animal behaviour **Values:** Rescuing and caring for animals **Critical thinking:** Share opinions about how our actions can affect animal habitats

How to use this book

In this book you will find lots of different features to help your learning.

What you will learn in the unit or lesson.

> **We are going to...**
> * **talk about our personalities**

Big questions to find out what you know already.

> **Getting started**
>
> Where would be an ideal place to live?
> a Look carefully at these optical illusion pictures.
>   What different landscapes can you see?
> b What's curious about them?
> c What can you see in the sky?
> d Discuss where you'd prefer to live. In the country?
>   In the mountains? By the sea? In the city? Give a reason why.

The key words feature includes vocabulary from other subjects, Academic English terms and command words.

> **Key words: Diet**
>
> calcium: is good for your bones.
> fibre: helps you to digest food properly.
> protein: helps your body to grow and build muscles.
> vitamins and minerals: give you healthy hair and skin.

Read real texts with helpful glossaries

> **Glossary**
>
> twirl: turn around quickly
> frilly: decorative material on a dress or skirt
> itch: rub or scratch your skin with your nails

Language detective boxes help you find out more about the main grammar in a unit.

> **Use of English – Past simple regular and irregular verbs**
>
> My grandad **rode** his bike to work.
> He **lived** in a wooden house.
> We don't add -ed to irregular verbs.
> He rode his bike to work.

Helps you remember other grammar.

> **Language focus**
>
> **Inferring**
>
> Inferring is making a guess or prediction about something you have some clues about.
>
> It could be a...because ...
> Perhaps, it's a...because...
> I can make out a...I think, because...

Tips you can use to
help you with your learning.

Speaking tip

Make notes

Make short notes to help you when
you are giving a presentation – don't
read your text word for word. Practise
and look at your classmates when you
are speaking.

At the end of each unit,
there is a choice of projects
to work on together, using
what you have learned.
You might do some research
or make something.

> 6.6 Project challenge

Project A: Create an Aboriginal dot painting for a class mural

1 What can you see in this painting? Use the symbols on page 97 to describe
   the scene or the story.

2 Plan your painting. Decide on the following:
   • Think about the scene or story it is going to tell.
   • Decide on the symbols you want to use.
   • Think about a title for your painting.
   • Organise the things you will need – card/paper, coloured pencils or paints.

3 First, sketch out your scene in pencil.

Questions to help you think about
how you learn.

How well did your group work together on your project?

This is what you have learned
in the unit.

Look what I can do

Write or show examples in your notebook.

I can compare and talk about the city and the country.
I can draw a 3D optical illusion.
I can use the past simple to talk about places in the past.
I can write a description about a fictional place.
I can understand a story about *The Lost City*.

Check your progress 1

1 **Read the clues and guess the words.**
   a This adjective describes someone who studies hard.
   b This is when your head hurts.
   c This is something we walk over to cross a road safely.
   d This is good for your bones.
   e This adjective describes someone who talks a lot.
   f This is something which controls the traffic.
   g This helps your muscles to grow.
   h This is the opposite of outgoing.
   i This adjective means very big.

Games and activities that
cover what you have learned
in the previous 3 units. If you
can answer these, you are
ready to move on to the
next unit.

Audio is available with the Digital Learner's Book, the Teacher's Resource or Digital Classroom

Video is available with Digital Classroom

How to use this book: Teacher

Lesson 1: The Think about it lesson introduces the topic through topic vocabulary activities

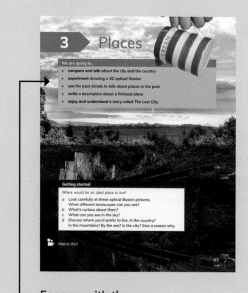

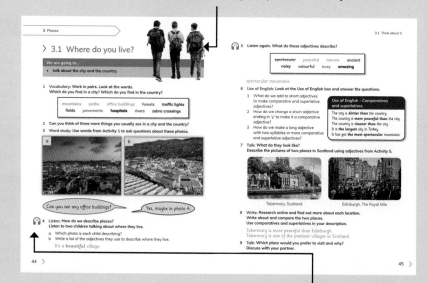

Engage with the topic of the unit and generate discussion using the image, the video and the big question.

The opening lesson includes listening.

Lesson 2: The cross-curricular lesson prepares learners to learn in English across the curriculum.

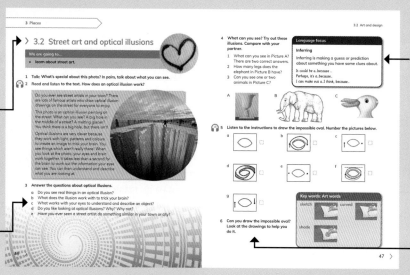

In this lesson you'll find Language focus and key words boxes.

A non-fiction text exposes learners to cross-curricular language.

There will be opportunities to think critically about the information in the text.

Lesson 3: The Talk about it lesson develops learners' speaking skills.

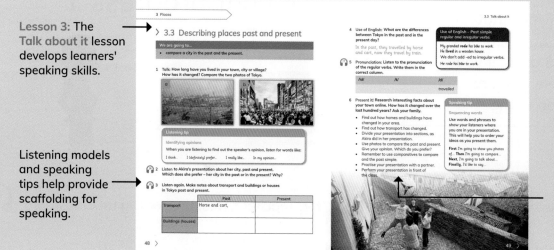

Listening models and speaking tips help provide scaffolding for speaking.

Pronunciation is supported through paired activities

Lesson 4: The Write about it section supports learners to write effective texts.

Model texts with callouts support the writing process.

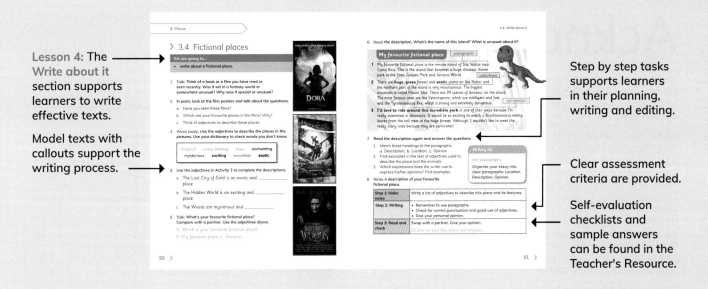

Step by step tasks supports learners in their planning, writing and editing.

Clear assessment criteria are provided.

Self-evaluation checklists and sample answers can be found in the Teacher's Resource.

Lesson 5: The Read and Respond lesson includes literature. This might be a fictional story, a poem or a play.

The audio can be played the first time you meet the story, before learners read the text.

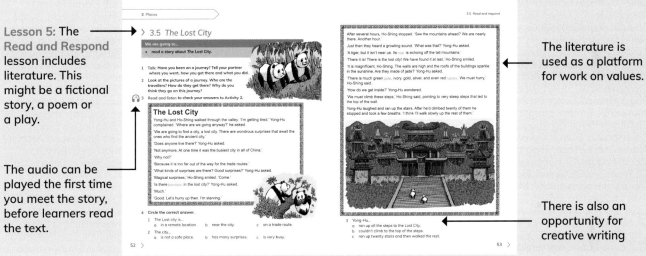

The literature is used as a platform for work on values.

There is also an opportunity for creative writing

Lesson 6: The Project challenge lesson includes choice of projects.

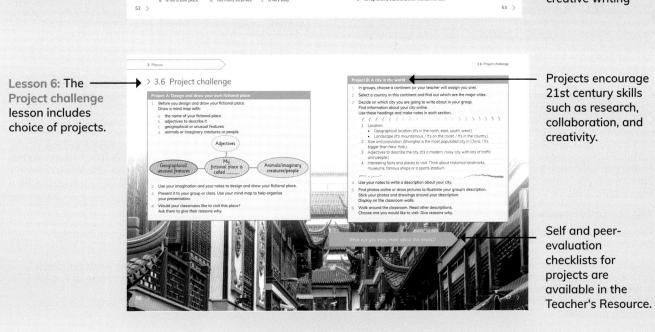

Projects encourage 21st century skills such as research, collaboration, and creativity.

Self and peer-evaluation checklists for projects are available in the Teacher's Resource.

Acknowledgements

The authors and publishers acknowledge the following sources of copyright material and are grateful for the permissions granted. While every effort has been made, it has not always been possible to identify the sources of all the material used, or to trace all copyright holders. If any omissions are brought to our notice, we will be happy to include the appropriate acknowledgements on reprinting.

Unit 1 'Our teacher's multi-talented' by Kenn Nesbitt, used with the permission of the author; 'Super Samson Simpson' from *Something Big Has Been Here* by Jack Prelutsky illustrated by James Stevenson. TEXT COPYRIGHT © 1990 BY JACK PRELUTSKY, ILLUSTRATIONS COPYRIGHT © 1990 BY JAMES STEVENSON Used by permission of HarperCollins Publishers; **Unit 3** 'The Lost City' by Margo Fallis, used and adapted with permission from the author; **Unit 4** Text and illustrations from *Horrid Henry's Birthday Party* by Francesca Simon, illustrations by Tony Ross, reproduced by permission of Orion Children's Books, an imprint of Hachette Children's Books, Carmelite House, 50 Victoria Embankment, London imprint, EC4Y 0DZ; **Unit 5** Extracts and illustrations from The Girl Who Thought in Pictures: The story of Dr Temple Grandin by Julia Finley Mosca, illustrations by Daniel Rieley, © 2017 The Innovation Press; **Unit 6** Excerpts from *The Little Prince* by Antoine De Saint-Exupery translated by Richard Howard, reprinted by permission of Houghton Mifflin Harcourt Publishing Company, illustrations and audio use © Editions Gallimard: **Unit 7** 'Horatius at the Bridge' James Baldwin; **Unit 8** 'A visit with Mr. Tree Frog' and 'If I were a sloth' by Kathy Paysen from her *Rainbows in the Rainforest Collection*; **Unit 9** 'Mum Won't Let Me Keep a Rabbit' from *Gargling with Jelly* by Brian Patten (Viking, 1985) Copyright© Brian Patten, 1985 and Reproduced by permission of the author c/o Rogers, Coleridge & White Ltd., and Penguin Random House UK.

Thanks to the following for permission to reproduce images:

Cover by Pablo Gallego (Beehive Illustration); Inside Unit 1 Mohd Hafiez Mohd Razali/GI; Jose Luis Pelaez Inc/GI; Planet Flem/GI; calvindexter/GI; Kelvin Murray/GI; Alistair Berg/GI; Kelvin Murray/GI; Alistair Berg/GI; Manfred Gottschalk/GI; Mixetto/GI; Adie Bush/GI; Adie Bush/GI; Kali9/GI; Jose Luis Pelaez Inc/GI; Jose Luis Pelaez Inc/GI; Hraun/GI; Ian Thwaites/Alamy Stock Photo; PhotoAlto/Sigrid Olsson/GI; RichVintage/GI; PhotoAlto/Sigrid Olsson/GI; Katelyn Mulcahy/GI; Westend61/GI; Jim Cummins/GI; Sorrapong Apidech/GI; Richard Newstead/GI; Unit 2 krisanapong detraphiphat/GI; Westend61/GI; Mrs/GI; filadendron/GI; Blend Images-JGI/Jamie Grill/GI; Jose Luis Pelaez Inc/GI; Claudia Totir/GI; RapidEye/GI; Jose Luis Pelaez Inc/GI; Claudia Totir/GI; RapidEye/GI; flybydust/GI; Madmaxer/GI; Tito Atchaa/GI; Photo and Co/GI; South China Morning Post/GI; Clerkenwell/GI; Stuart Minzey/GI; Fuse/GI; Clerkenwell/GI; Stuart Minzey/GI; Fuse/GI; Lew Robertson/GI; Lew Robertson/GI; ROGER HARRIS/SCIENCE PHOTO LIBRARY/GI; Roger Harris/Science Photo Librar/GI; Unit 3 Landscapes, Seascapes, Jeweller & Action Photography/GI; Artur Debat/GI; Cavan Images/GI; Tanatat pongphibool ,thailand/GI; F.J. Jimenez/Gi; e55evu/GI; Xavier Arnau Serrat/GI; Image Source/GI; Getty Images/GI; GeorgePeters/GI; Image Source/GI; GeorgePeters/GI; MeijiShowa/Alamy Stock Photo; TommL/GI; Enrico Calderoni/GI; Enrico Calderoni/GI; Everett Collection Inc/Alamy Stock Photo; NINA PROMMER/EPA-EFE/Shutterstock; PictureLux/The Hollywood Archive/Alamy Stock Photo; Thomas Winz/GI; Thomas Winz/GI; luxizeng/GI; Luxizeng/GI; Tanatat pongphibool,thailand/GI; e55evu/GI; Morsa Images/GI; aabejon/GI; Unit 4 ferrantraite/GI; South China Morning Post/GI; Tim Macpherson/GI; Roberto Soncin Gerometta/GI; Travel Ink/GI; Global_Pics/GI; Fuse/GI; ZUMA Press, Inc./Alamy Stock Photo; Getty Images/GI; DANIEL LEAL-OLIVAS/GI; Sergio Mendoza Hochmann/GI; SOPA Images/GI; Jeremy Woodhouse/GI; jane/GI; Westend61/GI; Asia Images Group/GI; Westend61/GI; Asia Images Group/GI; 500px Asia/GI; vinhdav/GI; Christine Müller/GI; Richard Hutchings/GI; Erika Eros/GI; Richard Hutchings/GI; Erika Eros/GI; DigiPub/GI; Ana Silva/GI; DigiPub/GI; Ana Silva/GI; Unit 5 Steve Russell/GI; Steve Russell/GI; Roberto Machado Noa/GI; JGI/GI; JGI/Tom Grill/GI; Image Source/GI; Image Source/GI; Ilyabolotov/GI; Aja Koska/GI; Dp_photo/GI; Dp_photo/GI; Unit 6 Rich Legg/GI; YASSER AL-ZAYYAT/GI; Fstop123/GI; Thomas Lai Yin Tang/GI; Universal History Archive/GI; Catherine Falls Commercial/GI; Catherine Falls Commercial/GI; Transcendental Graphics/GI; Frank Rothe/GI; Jordan Lye/GI; Westend61/GI; dedoma/Shutterstock; Peter Unger/GI; Peter Unger/GI; 130920/GI; Nattaya Mahaum/GI; Nattaya Mahaum/GI; Unit 7 Kenneth Alan Brown/GI; Miguel Sanz/GI; danbreckwoldt/GI; LianeM/GI; Harold M. Lambert/GI; x-drew/GI; Izzet Keribar/GI; FotografiaBasica/GI; Izzet Keribar/GI; FotografiaBasica/GI; Skaman306/GI; THEPALMER/GI; Fred Bahurlet/GI; Zhengjie Wu/GI; By Eve Livese/GI; Alexander Spatari/GI; Duncan1890/GI; Skaman306/GI; THEPALMER/GI; Fred Bahurlet/GI; By Eve Livesey/GI; Cyrille Gibot/GI; LianeM/GI; ChiccoDodiFC/GI; Grant Faint/GI; Harold M. Lambert/GI; Unit 8 Suttipong Sutiratanachai/GI; Rebecca Yale/GI; Ivan Cano/GI; By Marc Guitard/GI; by Marc Guitard/GI; DEA/G. SIOEN/GI; Majority World/GI; Pawel Opaska/GI; Pawel Opaska/GI; Getty Images/GI; David Marsden/GI; Dendeimos/GI; kozyrskyi/GI; Eduardo Fonseca Arraes/GI; Mohd Haniff Abas/GI; AFP/GI; Arun Roisri/GI; Ghislain & Marie David De Lossy/GI; lunamarina/Shutterstock; dawnanderson419/GI; KTSDESIGN/GI; Rebecca Yale/GI; kozyrskyi/GI; Harry Collins/GI; Unit 9 Carolyn Cole/GI; Wang He/GI; Javier Zayas/GI; Arthur Morris/GI; acceptfoto/GI; KeithSzafranski/GI; Chase Dekker Wild-Life Images/GI; Westend61/GI; Gado Images/GI; Mark Hamblin/GI; fototrav/GI; Juan Buitrago/GI; Giordano Cipriani/GI; Mark Webster/GI; Tim Graham/GI; Remanz/GI; Westend61/GI; George Karbus Photography/GI; Mike Brinson/GI; Shene/GI; track5/GI; George Karbus Photography/GI; Mike Brinson/GI; Shene/GI; Track5/GI; ROMEO GACAD/GI; Godong/GI; TOBIAS SCHWARZ/GI; Istvan Kadar Photography/GI; Vicki Jauron, Babylon and Beyond Photography/GI; Istvan Kadar Photography/GI; Vicki Jauron, Bab lon And Beond Photography/GI; JLewisPhoto/GI; Rob Maynard/GI; Rob Maynard/GI; Paul Souders/GI; SolStock/GI; Iaroshenko/GI; kiszon pascal/GI; Mike Hill/GI; SolStock/GI; Westend61/GI; kali9/GI

Key: GI = Getty Images

The authors and publishers would like to thank the following for reviewing Stage 5: Fariha Abbas, Marwati Saring, and Nidhi Chopra.

Development of this publication has made use of the Cambridge English Corpus (CEC). The CEC is a multi-billion word computer database of contemporary spoken and written English. It includes British English, American English and other varieties of English. It also includes the Cambridge Learner Corpus, developed in collaboration with Cambridge Assessment English. Cambridge University Press has built up the CEC to provide evidence about language use that helps to produce better language teaching materials.

1 ▶ Talking about people

We are going to...

- **talk** about our personalities
- **read** about people who protect the environment and help others
- **use** adjectives + prepositions to express how we feel about something
- **interview** our partners about their lives
- **write** about an inspirational person
- **enjoy** poems about special people.

Getting started

What personal qualities do we like to see in other people?

a   Describe the personality you can see in each picture.
b   Which pictures show positive personal qualities and which show negative ones?
c   Can you see yourself in any of these pictures?

 Watch this!

〉 1.1 What are you like?

We are going to...

* **talk about personalities.**

I think I'm outgoing because...

1 Write **three adjectives to describe yourself.**
Then share them with a partner. How similar are you?

2 Vocabulary: Can you find these personality types
in the picture? What helps you to decide?

cheerful   nervous   selfish   shy   talkative   hardworking

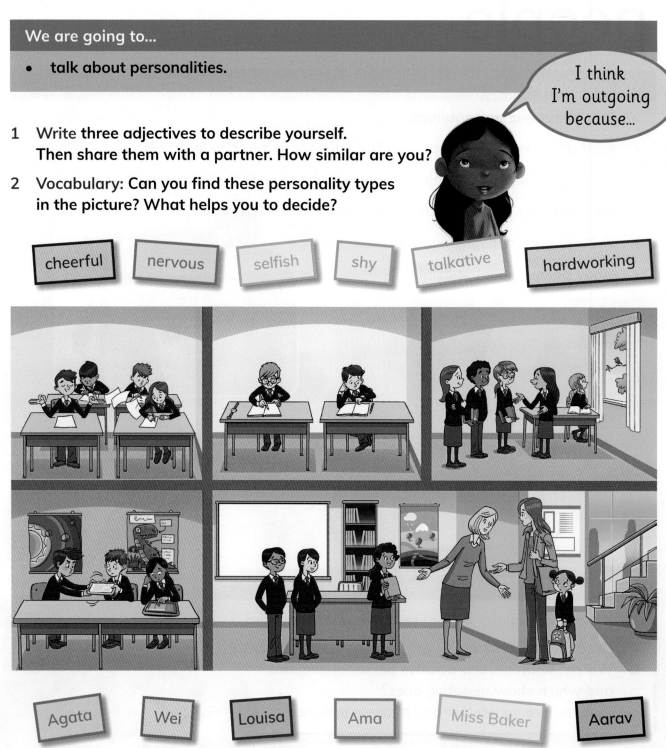

Agata   Wei   Louisa   Ama   Miss Baker   Aarav

3 **Listen** and match each name to someone in the picture.

Listening tip

Listen for specific information

Listen to identify specific information like names and adjectives.

4 **Complete the sentences with the correct adjective. Listen again and write the names.**

a   She always gets so _____ when we do tests in class. ___Agata___

b   He never stops talking. He's very _____. _____

c   She doesn't share anything with any of her friends.
    She's very _____. _____

d   He studies very hard. He's _____. _____

e   She goes red when she talks to adults. She's very _____. _____

f   She's so _____. She's always smiling and laughing in class. _____

5 **Word study: Match the adjectives to their opposite meanings.
You can use a dictionary to help you.**

1	talkative	a	generous
2	hardworking	b	outgoing
3	shy	c	bad-tempered
4	selfish	d	nervous
5	cheerful	e	lazy
6	calm	f	quiet

6 **In pairs, use opposite adjectives to compare your friends in class.**

Petra is very quiet in class...

...but Ravi is the opposite. He's very talkative.

7 **Write a short description about someone you know using the adjectives above. Give examples.**

My best friend's name is Sofia.
She's very hardworking and always
gets good grades in class.

⟩ 1.2 Make our world a better place!

We are going to...

- **read about people who protect the environment and help others**

1 **Talk: Work in pairs. Ask and answer these questions.**

  a Are you worried about your local environment?
     What problems are there?
  b How do people help others in your community?
  c How are animals and endangered species
     protected in your area?

02 2 **Read and listen: How are these people doing
     things for the community?**

Key words: Measurement

amount: the quantity of
something
estimate: to calculate the
size of something
immense: extremely big
size: how big something is

← → C ☆ ≡

Man walks backwards 700 km miles to protect rainforest

Medi Bastoni is walking backwards for 700 km because he is
worried about the destruction of the rainforests in his country.
Indonesia has 16 000 islands and most are covered by immense
rainforests. Deforestation is happening where he lives and he
thinks that they will disappear if they are not protected and
rebuilt. Rainforests are so important because they absorb carbon
emissions from our industries and vehicles and provide a habit for
many endangered species. Scientists are **shocked by** the destruction
and estimate that the amount of the world's rainforests that have disappeared are
almost twice the size of Japan.

Warming up the community

When Emma Burkhart was 9 years old she received two blankets
as presents and it gave her an idea. Emma was **interested in**
community projects and helping others. She thought there were
children and elderly people who needed the blankets more than
her, so she started to collect them. The first year she collected
200 blankets, which she was very **pleased with**. Last year, she
collected 900 new blankets! This year she is **excited about** collecting
even more for different organisations in her local community.

3   **Read the texts again and answer the questions.**

    a   Why do you think Medi chose to walk backwards?
       Do you think it's difficult?
    b   What is deforestation?
    c   Why is it important to rebuild the rainforests?
    d   What was Emma's community project?
    e   Why do you think elderly people and children
       might need the blankets?
    f   Have you ever done a physical challenge
       for charity?

> **Use of English – Adjectives and prepositions**
>
> He is **worried about** the destruction of the rainforests. Emma was **interested in** community projects.

4   **Use of English: Look at the Use of English box. Find similar patterns in the text.**

5   **How do these news reports make you feel? Tell your partner using these words.**

interested in   worried about   happy about   sad about

excited about   curious about   ready to

6   **How can you become an active citizen? Look at the topics below and choose one. Do a short presentation. Use the notes below to help you.**

Animal protection   Environmental issues   Helping people in the community

    a   Talk about why you are interested in this topic and why.

       I'm interested in animal protection because some people don't look after their pets very well.

    b   Talk about how you feel.

       I'm worried about pets that don't have a home.

    c   Talk about what you are going to do.

       I'm going to raise money for animal shelters by…

⟩ 1.3 Interviewing a friend

We are going to...

- interview our partner about their life.

1 Talk: Have you ever had an interview in English? How did you feel? What did you talk about?

 2 Listen to Ben having an interview with his English teacher. Order the topics he talks about.

a	family	_1_
b	friends	___
c	favourite things	___
d	personality	___
e	sports	___
f	school	___

 3 Listen again. Are the sentences **true** or **false**?

a	Ben has got an older brother called Max.	_False_
b	He is really outgoing.	___
c	He's known Micky for a long time.	___
d	He thinks he's good at drawing.	___
e	He's not keen on playing tennis.	___
f	His favourite things are his video games console and his collection of comics.	___

4 Vocabulary: Match the useful expressions in the Speaking tip box with the correct category below.

a	Check for meaning	_3_
b	Correcting yourself	___
c	Expressing likes and dislikes	___
d	Comparing	___
e	Expressing opinions	___

> **Speaking tip**
>
> Useful expressions for speaking
>
> 1 I really like...
> 2 It makes me (happy)
> 3 Sorry, could you repeat that?
> 4 What I meant was...
> 5 I'm not very keen on...
> 6 I don't think...
> 7 We both play...
> 8 I'm not sure if...

5 Listen and write the questions.

 6 Pronunciation: Listen again and mark the intonation.
Then listen again and repeat.

What are you like?

Use of English – Present simple

We use the present simple to talk about states, routines and habits.

He **is** really cheerful and fun to be with. (state)
I **start** school at 9 o'clock every day. (routine)
I always **play** online at the weekends. (habit)

---

7 Use of English: Are these sentences examples
of states or routines? Mark (S) or (R).

a I'm good at singing.   _____
b I play tennis twice a week.   _____
c I'm a bit shy.   _____
d I sometimes take part in competitions.   _____

8 In pairs, prepare for an interview.

a Make notes about your life using the topics from Activity 2.

  Family: I've got a brother and two sisters.

  Friends: Kiara is my best friend.

b Write questions about each of these topics to ask your partner.

  Family: Have you got any brothers or sisters? How old are they?

  Friends: Who is your best friend? Why is he/she your best friend?

c Interview your partner.
  Remember to use the useful
  expressions in the Speaking tip.

1.4 Role models

We are going to...

- write about an inspirational person.

1 **Talk: Do you have any role models (a family member, someone in your community or a famous person)? Why are they role models for you?**

2 **What does 'chase your dreams' mean? Look at the photo. Who and what do you think this text is about?**

Chase your dreams!

I'm Eva and I have autism. Chase is a role model for me. Read to find out why.

a state

1 Chase is **a young cookbook author** and YouTube star. Cooking is his passion. It started when he was watching a cooking channel on the TV with his grandfather. He became a fan of the programme and told his mum he wanted to try cooking. He went to restaurants for the first time and tried new kinds of foods. Now, **Chase watches cooking shows every day** for inspiration. He tries new recipes every week, and likes to learn about the food people eat around the world.

a routine

2 When he was 15 he wrote his first cookbook, which is full of tasty recipes and fun facts about food. He also has a YouTube cooking programme. He records a new show every Friday. They are very funny, especially when guest chefs visit the show!

3 Chase is autistic. When he was very young he didn't like food very much. In fact he only ate five types of food. Speaking is also a challenge because he has to think about the order of the words before he speaks, but Chase knows he's a good cook and he loves being in the kitchen! He is very confident and creative and his shows are very funny too!

personality

4 He hopes his cookbook will inspire other children who have a dream. His message is, 'Always focus on the things you're good at – your abilities, not your disabilities.' He's also excited about his *Chase your dreams foundation* to help other children who live with autism. In the future he would like his own cooking show and he wants to open five different types of restaurant.

adjective + preposition

3 **Read the text and answer the questions.**

  a   Why do you think Chase is a role model
        for lots of children?
  b   What is he like?
  c   What challenges has he overcome?
  d   What plans does he have for the future?

Writing tip

Proof read your work.

Read your work again
and check it for errors.

4 **Match these headings to the paragraphs in the text.**

Achievements   Background   An inspiration   Challenges and personality

5 **Write a description about an inspirational person.**

Step 1: Research and planning	Find information about your role model on the internet or in magazines (or interview a family member) and make notes under the headings below.
	1 Background 2 Achievements 3 Personality and challenges 4 An inspiration
Step 2: Writing	Remember to use the present simple to talk about routines, states and habits. You could use some adjectives with prepositions too: He/she is **good at**... He/she is **interested in**...
Step 3: Read and check	Swap with a partner. Proof read your partner's work. Circle where you think there are errors and give back to your partner to correct.

6 **Now you have finished your description.**
Check you have included everything on the checklist.

Checklist ✓

Use paragraphs.   ☐
Use the present simple to write about states, routines and habits. ☐
Read and check your writing.   ☐
Add a photo.   ☐

> 1.5 My favourite people

We are going to...

- enjoy poems about special people.

1 **Talk:** Who inspires you? What is special about them? Discuss in pairs.

 2 **Read and listen** to the two poems by Kenn Nesbit. Match a name to each one.

Title 1: Our teacher's multi-talented by Kenn Nesbit

Title 2: Super Samson Simpson by Jack Prelutsky

Poem A

1 I am _____
I'm superlatively strong,
I like to carry elephants,
I do it all day long,
5 I pick up half a dozen
and hoist them in the
air, it's really somewhat
simple, for I have
strength to spare.

10 My muscles are
enormous, they bulge
from top to toe, and
when I carry elephants,
they ripple to and fro,
15 but I am not the
strongest in the
Simpson family, for
when I carry elephants,
my grandma carries me.

Poem B

1 _____
He plays guitar and sings.
He paints impressive pictures
and can juggle twenty rings.

5 He dances like an expert,
he can mambo, tap and waltz.
He's also quite a gymnast,
doing airborne somersaults.

He's something of a swimmer.
10 He's a champion at chess.
It's difficult to find a skill
that he does not possess.

He speaks a dozen languages.
He's great at racing cars.
15 He's masterful at fighting bulls,
and studying the stars.

He's good at climbing mountains.
He can wrestle with a bear.
The only thing we wish he'd learn
20 Is how to comb his hair.

3 Match the illustrations with lines from the poems.

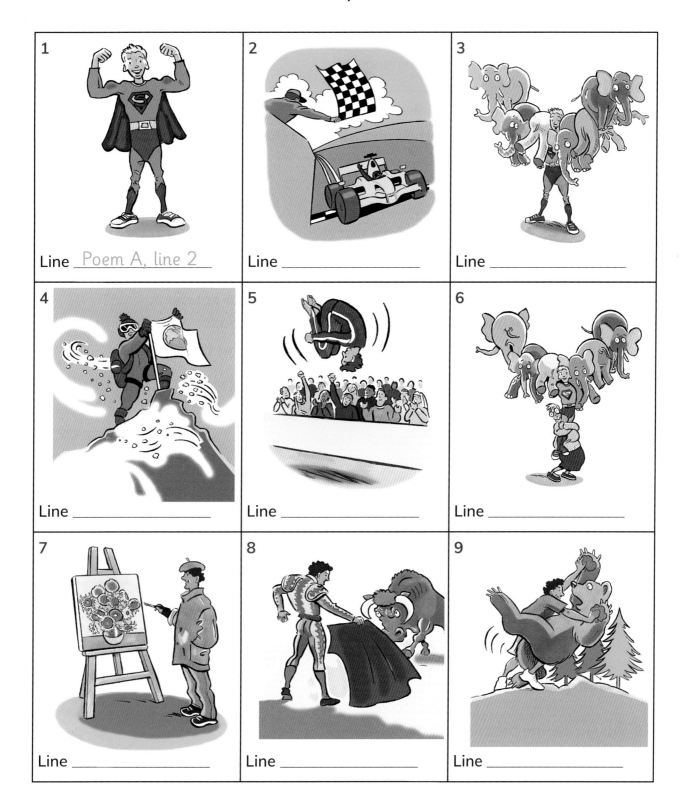

1 Line _Poem A, line 2_

2 Line _____

3 Line _____

4 Line _____

5 Line _____

6 Line _____

7 Line _____

8 Line _____

9 Line _____

4 Tick (✓) the correct sentences and cross (✗) the incorrect sentences.

a Super Samson Simpson is good at carrying elephants. _____

b He's not good at carrying his grandma. _____

c The teacher isn't good at painting. _____

d He's very good at chess. _____

e He isn't good at swimming. _____

5 Word study: Match these definitions with the red words in the poems in Activity 2.

a twelve of something _____

b very big _____

c a winner of something _____

d to fight _____

e to lift up _____

f special, important _____

6 Read poem B again. Find and write the phrases in your notebook that mean to be good at something.

7 Word study: Use your dictionary to write a definition for these words.

a impressive   b to comb   c to juggle   d to carry   e to bulge   f an expert

8 Talk: With a partner, take turns to read your definitions for the other partner to guess.

9 Complete this poem about your role model.

An Inspirational Person
He/She can...
He/She's also quite a...
He/She's something of a...
He/She's a champion at...
He/She's great at...
He/She's masterful at...
He/She's good at...

10 Values: Be the best form of ourselves!

What are your personal qualities? Do you have any negative ones?

What are your special abilities?

Write notes about 'The Best Me'. Compare with a partner.

11 Match the words from the poems that rhyme. Then listen and check.

air rings possess strong stars
long me chess
cars family sings spare

12 Choose words from the box to complete the verse about an inspirational person below, or use your own ideas.

| the | guitar | three | languages | driving | cars | archery |

She speaks more than ..,
She's good at playing...,
She's masterful at...,
And not bad at...

> 1.6 Project challenge

Project A: Design a motivational poster for your classroom

1 Read these quotes. What you think they mean? Talk with your group.

> 1 If you think someone needs a friend, be one!

> 2 Today is a great day to learn something new!

> 3 Believe in yourself, you can do it!

> 4 No one is perfect, that's why pencils have rubbers!

2 Match the quotes to the pictures.

a

c

b

d

3 Which quote do you like best? Why do you like it?

4 In pairs, research online to find a motivational quote you like about learning and life.

- Vote in your group on the one you like best.
- Draw a picture to illustrate the quote.
- Write the quote in large, colourful writing on a piece of card.
- Stick the picture under the quote.
- Display on the classroom walls for everyone to read and think about.

Project B: Special people

1   First, organise yourselves into groups of four or five.

2   You need a roll of paper big enough to draw the outline of a volunteer's body on the floor. (If you don't have paper you can use chalk instead.)

3   Think about a special person in your life. It could be a family member, a friend or someone in your community.

    Think about why they are special. Think of the personal qualities they have.

4   Each person in the group needs a different coloured pen or piece of chalk.

    Write the qualities this person has on the outline of the body. Don't write the name of the person.

5   Present this person to the group. Point to the personal qualities you have written as you tell your group why this person is special.

How well did your group work together on your project?

> 1.7 What do you know now?

What personal qualities do we like in other people?

1 What are the opposites of these adjectives?

bad-tempered shy calm generous hardworking

4 Practise the intonation of the questions above. Remember to use an up-fall intonation.

2 Write down three adjectives to describe yourself. Compare with your partner. Give reasons.
I think I'm _____ because...

5 Use the present simple to talk about two of your daily routines and two states. For example: **What are you like?**

7 Write words that rhyme with:
**light   day   true
past   bring**

3 Write six questions to ask your partner about their life using:
**What   Which   Who
When   Where   Why**

6 Complete the sentences for you.
**I'm happy about...
I'm worried about...
I'm interested in...
I'm excited about...**

Look what I can do

Write or show examples in your notebook.

I can talk about personalities.

I can read and understand articles about people who protect the environment and help others.

I can use adjectives + prepositions to express how I feel about something.

I can interview my partner about their life.

I can write about an inspirational person.

I can read and understand poems about special people.

2 Food and health

We are going to...

- **talk** about common illnesses and their symptoms
- **understand a text** about a healthy diet
- **give** a presentation about protection from insect bites
- **use** modal verbs to give advice to our classmates
- **write** a post for the class health blog
- **enjoy and understand** a world folktale called *Stone Soup.*

Getting started

How can we live healthy lives?

a   What food types can you see in the photos? Write them in 30 seconds!

b   Tick those you eat most. Compare with a partner.

c   Who eats the most healthily?

d   Discuss why it is important to have a healthy diet.

Watch this!

〉 2.1 What are common illnesses?

We are going to...

- talk about common illnesses and their symptoms.

1 **Talk:** What common illnesses have you had over the last year?
Are you ill more in the warm or cold weather?
What usually causes these common illnesses?

2 **Vocabulary:** Match the words with the correct pictures below. What word can't you find? Check its meaning in your dictionary.

| a sore throat a cough a cold earache a fever a headache stomach ache |

 3 Listen to the conversation with a doctor. Which illness is each child suffering from?

 4 Listen again and number the symptoms in the order that you hear them.

a no energy b lost voice c feel sick d shivering e head hurts
f runny nose g sweating h tummy hurts i chesty cough j blocked nose

5 **Read** the riddle. What is being described?

I am everywhere – on your door handle, the table, your keyboard, even on your skin! I don't eat and no one can see me, unless they have a microscope. If I get inside your body I can multiply and make you sick. I can give you anything from a simple cold to the flu or serious illnesses.

6 **What do viruses do to the body? Listen and write T (true) or F (false).**

a You can't see a virus with your own eyes. ___T___
b A virus has many different shapes. _____
c They always make you sick. _____
d They multiply when they enter a human cell.
e Your immune system can protect you from viruses. _____
f Fever can't protect you from the virus. _____

> ### Language focus – Indefinite pronouns
>
> We use indefinite pronouns such as, everyone, everywhere and everything to refer to people, places and things without saying exactly who or what they are.
>
> I am everywhere.

7 **Use of English: Can you find two more indefinite pronouns in the text in Activity 5?**

8 **Write: How can you prevent getting a virus? Write a caption for these pictures.**

9 **Talk: What three new things have you learned about viruses? Compare your ideas with a partner.**

> 2.2 The food plate

We are going to...

- find out about healthy food.

1   **Vocabulary: Do you eat a healthy diet? What do you know about food?**
    Look at the food plate and follow these instructions. Compare with a partner.

a   Find a food that you eat every day.

b   Find two products made from milk.

c   Find a fruit and vegetable that you like.

d   Find a food that you don't like.

- Fruit and vegetables
- Grains, cereals and potatoes
- Dairy products
- Meat, fish, nuts and eggs
- Fats and sugars

 2   **Read and listen: Why is it important to eat a balanced diet? Match the**
    headings in Activity 1 to the parts of the text A–E. Then listen and check.

a   These are made with milk. They contain calcium, which is good for both bones and teeth. Yoghurt and cheese are examples of these products too.

b   These are good for us because they give our bodies energy. There are lots of grains to choose from, including brown rice, corn, wheat and oats.

c   This type of foods contains protein and helps your body to grow and build muscles.

d   We don't eat as many of these as we should! All vegetables contain vitamins and minerals that give us healthy hair and skin. They also contain fibre, which helps you to digest food properly. Make sure you eat whole fruit and don't drink as much fruit juice because it has a lot of sugar, which isn't good for you!

e   We should eat foods with less salt and sugar, and we should drink fewer soft drinks too.

Key words: Diet

calcium: is good for your bones.
fibre: helps you to digest food properly.
protein: helps your body to grow and build muscles.
vitamins and minerals: give you healthy hair and skin.

Use of English – Quantifiers

A quantifier expresses quantity.

Countable nouns:

We should drink **fewer** soft drinks.
We don't eat **as many** of these as we should!

Uncountable nouns:

We should eat foods with **less** salt and sugar.
Make sure you eat whole fruit and don't drink as **much** fruit juice.
Calcium is good for **both** bones and teeth.
All vegetables contain vitamins.

3   Use of English: Find and circle all the quantifiers in the text on page 30.

4   Talk: Imagine you are giving advice to children younger than you.
    Tell them about healthy eating. Use quantifiers and these words to help you.

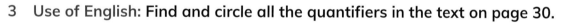

| muscles | protein | energy | bones |

| vitamins | dairy products | grains | calcium |

5   Work in a small group. Design a healthy food plate.
    Think about how different types of food help you
    throughout the day.

Brown rice or bread is good because grains give
you energy.

❯ 2.3 Mosquitoes and malaria

We are going to...

- use modal verbs to talk about mosquitoes and malaria.

1   What is this insect? What do you know about it? Add more facts of your own.

It likes hot weather.

It makes a buzzing sound.

 2   Listen to Nala talking about mosquitoes. Check your ideas in Activity 1. Why is the mosquito the most dangerous insect for humans on the planet?

 3   Listen again and match the headings to the mosquito fact file.

> ~~number of species~~   diet   lifespan   curious fact
> habitat   climate   **Mosquito dangers**

1 *Number of species*	More than 3,500
2	They usually live near water, such as ponds, lakes and puddles of rain water, where the females lay their eggs
3	Nectar from fruit and plants; blood (females only)
4	Warm, wet weather
5	They can cause serious illnesses
6	Less than one month
7	Only females bite us

 4   Pronunciation: Listen and repeat the words. Where is the main stress in each word?

mosquitoes   repellent   malaria   environment

5 Vocabulary: How can we protect ourselves from mosquitoes? Match the words to the pictures.

a burn mosquito coils   b sleep under mosquito nets   c use insect repellent   d clean up your local environment

Use of English – Modal verbs

We can use modal verbs to give advice or to talk about obligation.

You **should** always use mosquito nets to protect you from mosquitoes when you sleep.

You **must** use an insect repellent.

Speaking tip

Make notes

Make short notes to help you when you are giving a presentation – don't read your text word for word. Practise and look at your classmates when you are speaking.

6 Use of English: Look at the Use of English box and use modals to talk about how to protect yourself from mosquito bites.

7 In pairs, prepare a presentation about bees. Find information online or in your library and make notes under these headings:

number of species   habitat   diet
climate   dangers   lifespan   curious fact

8 Draw pictures of bees or find photos on the internet. Take turns to present your information.

9 Find out about and give advice on how to avoid bee stings. Use modal verbs in your presentation.

You should stand still if a bee is buzzing around you.

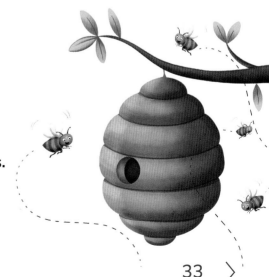

33

› 2.4 Health blogs

We are going to...

- **write a class health blog.**

1 Vocabulary: **Have you had an infection or an allergic reaction to food? Talk about the ones below with a partner.**

> **ear infection**   **allergic reaction**   a skin rash
> a chest infection   **a sore throat**   a cough

Have you ever had a...?

Yes, I have. / No, I haven't.

2 Read: **What kind of text is this? Who do you think the writers are?**

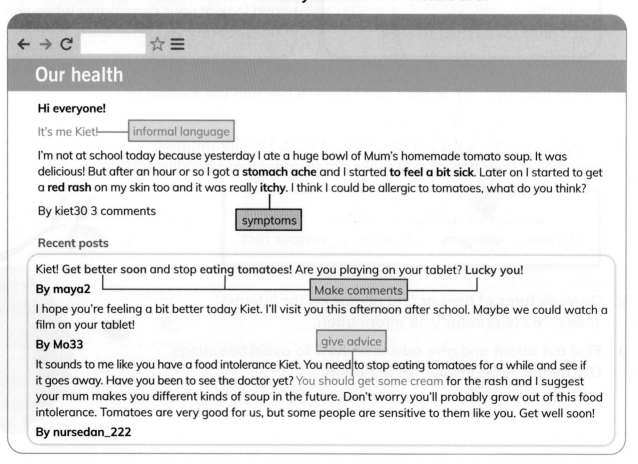

Our health

Hi everyone!

It's me Kiet! ——— informal language

I'm not at school today because yesterday I ate a huge bowl of Mum's homemade tomato soup. It was delicious! But after an hour or so I got a **stomach ache** and I started **to feel a bit sick**. Later on I started to get a **red rash** on my skin too and it was really **itchy**. I think I could be allergic to tomatoes, what do you think?

By kiet30 3 comments ——— symptoms

Recent posts

Kiet! Get better soon and stop eating tomatoes! Are you playing on your tablet? Lucky you!

By maya2 ——— Make comments

I hope you're feeling a bit better today Kiet. I'll visit you this afternoon after school. Maybe we could watch a film on your tablet!

By Mo33 ——— give advice

It sounds to me like you have a food intolerance Kiet. You need to stop eating tomatoes for a while and see if it goes away. Have you been to see the doctor yet? You should get some cream for the rash and I suggest your mum makes you different kinds of soup in the future. Don't worry you'll probably grow out of this food intolerance. Tomatoes are very good for us, but some people are sensitive to them like you. Get well soon!

By nursedan_222

3 Read the blog again and answer the questions.

    a   What's the matter with Kiet?

    b   What were his symptoms?

    c   What does Mo33 want to do after school?

    d   What do you think about the advice his friends give him?

4 Talk: Does your school or class have a blog? What can you use a blog for? How can it help your learning?

5 Write a blog post about when you were last ill.

Step 1: Planning	Think about when you were last ill or choose one of the common illnesses from Lesson 2.1. Make notes about: • how you felt • what symptoms you had • what you did on the day you were ill.
Step 2: Writing	Remember to use your plan and use some informal phrases.
Step 3: Read and respond	• Swap with 4–5 classmates. • Write comments. (Get well soon! I hope you're feeling better!) • Use modal verbs to give some advice. (You should keep warm. You need to drink lots of water. You must go to the doctor's for some medicine.)

6 Now you have finished your blog.
Check you have included everything on the checklist.

> **Checklist** ✓
>
> Write short, informal sentences. ☐
>
> Use modal verbs to give advice and
> to express obligation. ☐
>
> Give all the symptoms of your illness. ☐

7 Display or publish your work on the class or school blog.

❭ 2.5 Stone Soup, A world folktale

We are going to...

- enjoy a folktale.

1 **Talk: Look at ingredients for a soup below. Which one is odd?**

 2 **Read and listen to the story and check your answer to Exercise 1.**

Stone soup

Once there was a young man who was travelling around the country selling his **goods**. Times were very hard and everyday he sold less and less until he didn't have any money at all. On the same day that he ran out of money and food, he came across a small village. He thought that in the village he would find someone who would give him a bit of food.

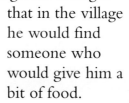

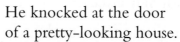

He knocked at the door of a pretty-looking house.
A woman opened the door slightly. The young man asked the woman if she had a little food to **spare** for a **weary**, young traveller, but sadly the woman answered that she had no food at all. Curiously, the same thing happened at all the houses in the village. There was not even a **crumb of bread** left in the entire village! The young man was not **discouraged**; instead he came up with a plan.

The young man found a wealthy-looking house in the centre of the village. An elderly man answered the door. The young man asked him if he had a large pot of water that he could spare. The old man asked him what he wanted it for. The young man explained that he was so sad about the lack of food in the village that he was going to make a big pot of soup for all the villagers from a special stone he had found on his travels.

The old man gave the young man a large pot of water and a stirring spoon and helped him build a big fire next to his house. The young man took a smooth stone out of his bag and put it in the pot of water. As he stirred the water, the young man mentioned to the old man that the magic soup is always better with a little onion and a head of cabbage to add extra flavour. So the old man went into his house and returned with a bag of onions and a head of cabbage.

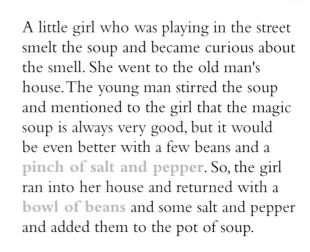

A little girl who was playing in the street smelt the soup and became curious about the smell. She went to the old man's house. The young man stirred the soup and mentioned to the girl that the magic soup is always very good, but it would be even better with a few beans and a pinch of salt and pepper. So, the girl ran into her house and returned with a bowl of beans and some salt and pepper and added them to the pot of soup.

The woman from the first house where the young man had asked for some food was in her garden collecting some herbs and mushrooms from her garden. She smelt the soup and became curious about the smell. So, she walked down the **lane** to the old man's house. The young man stirred the soup some more and mentioned that the magic soup is always very good, but that a few mushrooms and some herbs from her basket would add even more flavour. The woman gladly added her ingredients to the soup.

In a while the soup was cooked and everyone has a bowl of delicious stone soup. No one could believe that such a **flavoursome** soup could be made from just a stone. The young man served another bowl of soup and smiled to himself.

Glossary

goods: things that you have
spare: something available to use because it is extra and not being used
weary: tired
discouraged: to lose confidence
lane: a narrow road in a town or village
flavoursome: food that has a good taste

3 **Read: Answer the questions about the story.**

a   Why did the young man decide to make the stone soup?
b   What did the old man give him?
c   What ingredients did the people in the village give him for the stone soup?
d   How did he persuade the people in the village to give him the ingredients for his soup?
e   Why do you think the people in the village wouldn't give him any food when he arrived?
f   Why do you think the young man smiled to himself at the end of the story?
g   What value did the young man teach the people in the village that day?

4 Word study: **What words classify these items from the story? They are in** blue**.**

1 cabbage

2 salt and pepper

3 bread

4 beans

5 onions

Language focus

Classifying expressions

We use of when we talk about collections of items.

a crumb **of** bread

a pot **of** water

 5 Pronunciation: **Listen and repeat the phrases from the story with connected speech.**

1 a pot of water

2 a bunch of carrots

3 a pinch of salt and pepper

4 a bowl of beans

a What happens to of?

b Is it pronounced differently?

6 Values: **Helping each other**

a How do you help in your home or in your community?

b Look at the pictures and discuss how these children are helping in their home or community.

7 **Make a resolution.**

I'm going to...

> 2.6 Project challenge

Project A: Write a food diary for a week

1 Look at Omer's food diary for a week below.
Do you think he ate healthily this week?

	Sunday	Monday	Tuesday	Wednesday	Thursday	Friday	Saturday
Fats and sugars	★	★					
Meat, fish, eggs, nuts	★	★	★	★	★	★	★
Dairy products	★	★	★			★	
Grains, cereals and potatoes	★	★	★	★	★	★	★
Fruit and vegetables	★		★		★		

2 Work in pairs. Talk about how much food Omer ate from each food group.
Use some/any and quantifiers. Do you want to give him any advice?

He ate a lot of vegetables! He didn't eat any fish!

Omer, you need to eat more fruit!

Why don't you try a new vegetable?

3 Keep a food diary for a week.
Remember to fill it in every day at school or at home.

Project B: A common illness

1 Look at this cartoon and answer these questions.

7 days later

a What common illness has the boy got?

b What causes it?

c What symptoms can you have?

d How long can it last?

2 Now, divide into groups and brainstorm common illnesses that affect people in your country.

3 Decide on the illness your group is going to investigate.

4 Find information about it online and make notes using the questions in Activity 1 to help you.

5 Present your findings to the rest of the class. You could do a PowerPoint presentation with pictures or diagrams, or make a poster.

6 Tell another group about your findings.

What was the most interesting thing you found out doing this project?

› 2.7 What do you know now?

How can we live healthy lives?

1 Complete this list of common illnesses:
a sore throat...

4 Write down all the ways people can protect themselves from malaria

5 Write five sentences using these quantifiers.

less   all   both   fewer

not as much   not as many

2 Write the names of the nutrients our bodies need to keep us healthy.

3 Complete these food collocations. Write two more collocations of your own.
_____ **of onions**
_____ **of cabbage**

6 Give some health advice to your classmates.
You should eat more fruit.

Look what I can do

Write or show examples in your notebook.

I can talk about common illnesses and their symptoms.

I can understand a text about a healthy diet

I can give a presentation about protection from insect bites

I can use modal verbs to give advice to our classmates

I can write a post for the class health blog

I can enjoy and understand a world folktale.

3 ▶ Places

We are going to...

- **compare and talk** about the city and the country
- **experiment** drawing a 3D optical illusion
- **use** the past simple to talk about places in the past
- **write** a description about a fictional place
- **enjoy and understand** a story called *The Lost City*.

Getting started

Where would be an ideal place to live?

a   Look carefully at these optical illusion pictures.
    What different landscapes can you see?
b   What's curious about them?
c   What can you see in the sky?
d   Discuss where you'd prefer to live. In the country?
    In the mountains? By the sea? In the city? Give a reason why.

 Watch this!

〉 3.1 Where do you live?

We are going to...

- talk about the city and the country.

1 **Vocabulary: Work in pairs. Look at the words.**
Which do you find in a city? Which do you find in the country?

> mountains   paths   office buildings   forests   traffic lights
>
> fields   pavements   hospitals   rivers   zebra crossings

2 **Can you think of three more things you usually see in a city and the country?**

3 **Word study: Use words from Activity 1 to ask questions about these photos.**

Can you see any office buildings?

Yes, maybe in photo A.

4 **Listen: How do we describe places?**
Listen to two children talking about where they live.

a Which photo is each child describing?

b Write a list of the adjectives they use to describe where they live.

It's a **beautiful** village.

5 Listen again. What do these adjectives describe?

> ~~spectacular~~   peaceful   narrow   **ancient**
> **noisy**   **colourful**   busy   **amazing**

spectacular mountains

6 Use of English: Look at the Use of English box and answer the questions.

1 What do we add to short adjectives to make comparative and superlative adjectives?

2 How do we change a short adjective ending in 'y' to make it a comparative adjective?

3 How do we make a long adjective with two syllables or more comparative and superlative adjectives?

Use of English – Comparatives and superlatives

The city is **dirtier than** the country.
The country is **more peaceful than** the city.
The country is **cleaner than** the city.
It is **the largest** city in Turkey.
It has got **the most spectacula**r mountains.

7 Talk: What do they look like?
Describe the pictures of two places in Scotland using adjectives from Activity 5.

Tobermory, Scotland

Edinburgh, The Royal Mile

8 Write: Research online and find out more about each location.
Write about and compare the two places.
Use comparatives and superlatives in your description.

Tobermory is more peaceful than Edinburgh.
Tobermory is one of the prettiest villages in Scotland.

9 Talk: Which place would you prefer to visit and why?
Discuss with your partner.

〉 3.2 Street art and optical illusions

We are going to...

- **learn about street art.**

1 **Talk: What's special about this photo? In pairs, talk about what you can see.**

 2 **Read and listen to the text. How does an optical illusion work?**

Do you ever see street artists in your town? There are lots of famous artists who draw optical illusion drawings on the street for everyone to enjoy.

This photo is an optical illusion painting on the street. What can you see? A big hole in the middle of a street? A melting glacier? You think there is a big hole, but there isn't!

Optical illusions are very clever because they work with light, patterns and colours to create an image to trick your brain. You see things which aren't really there! When you look at the photo, your eyes and brain work together. It takes less than a second for the brain to work out the information your eyes can see. You can then understand and describe what you are looking at.

3 **Answer the questions about optical illusions.**

   a   Do you see real things in an optical illusion?
   b   What does the illusion work with to trick your brain?
   c   What works with your eyes to understand and describe an object?
   d   Do you like looking at optical illusions? Why? Why not?
   e   Have you ever seen a street artist do something similar in your town or city?

4 **What can you see? Try out these illusions. Compare with your partner.**

1 What can you see in Picture A? There are two correct answers.
2 How many legs does the elephant in Picture B have?
3 Can you see one or two animals in Picture C?

Language focus

Inferring

Inferring is making a guess or prediction about something you have some clues about.

It could be a...because ...
Perhaps, it's a...because...
I can make out a...I think, because...

A

B

C

🎧 15 5 **Listen to the instructions to draw the impossible oval. Number the pictures below.**

a 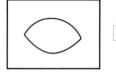 ☐

b 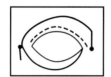 ☐

c 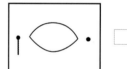 ☐

d  ☐

e 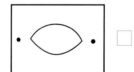 ☐

f 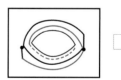 ☐

g 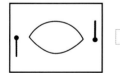 ☐

6 **Can you draw the impossible oval? Look at the drawings to help you do it.**

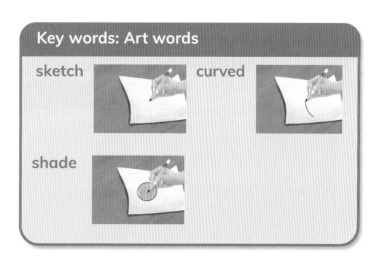

Key words: Art words

sketch

curved

shade

〉 3.3 Describing places past and present

We are going to...

- compare a city in the past and the present.

1 **Talk: How long have you lived in your town, city or village?
How has it changed? Compare the two photos of Tokyo.**

a

b

Listening tip

Identifying opinions

When you are listening to find out the speaker's opinion, listen for words like:

I think...   I (definitely) prefer...   I really like...   In my opinion...

---

 2 **Listen to Akira's presentation about her city, past and present.
Which does she prefer – her city in the past or in the present? Why?**

 3 **Listen again. Make notes about transport and buildings or houses
in Tokyo past and present.**

	Past	Present
Transport	Horse and cart,	
Buildings (houses)		

4 **Use of English: What are the differences between Tokyo in the past and in the present day?**

In the past, they travelled by horse and cart, now they travel by train.

> **Use of English – Past simple regular and irregular verbs**
>
> My grandad **rode** his bike to work.
>
> He **lived** in a wooden house.
>
> We don't add -ed to irregular verbs.
>
> He rode his bike to work.

17 **5** **Pronunciation: Listen to the pronunciation of the regular verbs. Write them in the correct column.**

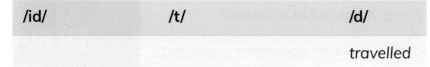

/id/	/t/	/d/
		travelled

6 **Present it! Research interesting facts about your town online. How has it changed over the last hundred years? Ask your family.**

- Find out how homes and buildings have changed in your area.
- Find out how transport has changed.
- Divide your presentation into sections, as Akira did in her presentation.
- Use photos to compare the past and present. Give your opinion. Which do you prefer?
- Remember to use comparatives to compare and the past simple.
- Practise your presentation with a partner.
- Perform your presentation in front of the class.

> **Speaking tip**
>
> Sequencing words
>
> Use words and phrases to show your listeners where you are in your presentation. This will help you to order your ideas as you present them.
>
> **First** I'm going to show you photos of... **Then** I'm going to compare... **Next**, I'm going to talk about... **Finally**, I'd like to say...

〉 3.4 Fictional places

We are going to...

- write about a fictional place.

1 **Talk: Think of a book or a film you have read or seen recently. Was it set in a fantasy world or somewhere unusual? Why was it special or unusual?**

2 **In pairs, look at the film posters and talk about the questions.**

 a Have you seen these films?

 b Which are your favourite places in the films? Why?

 c Think of adjectives to describe these places.

3 **Word study: Use the adjectives to describe the places in the pictures. Use your dictionary to check words you don't know.**

magical	scary-looking	huge	**enchanting**
mysterious	**exciting**	incredible	**exotic**

4 **Use the adjectives in Activity 3 to complete the descriptions.**

 a The Lost City of Gold is an exotic and _____ place.

 b The Hidden World is an exciting and _____ place.

 c The Woods are mysterious and _____ .

5 **Talk: What's your favourite fictional place? Compare with a partner. Use the adjectives above.**

 A: Which is your favourite fictional place?

 B: My favourite place is...because...

6 Read the description. What's the name of this island? What is unusual about it?

My favourite fictional place [paragraphs]

1 My favourite fictional place is the remote island of Isla Nublar near Costa Rica. This is the island that becomes a huge dinosaur theme park in the films Jurassic Park and Jurassic World. [adjectives]

2 There are **huge**, **green** forests and **exotic** plants on Isla Nubar and the northern part of the island is very mountainous. The biggest mountain is called Mount Sibo. There are 39 species of dinosaur on the island. The most famous ones are the Velociraptors, which are intelligent and fast, and the Tyrannosaurus Rex, which is strong and extremely dangerous. [an opinion]

3 **I'd love to ride around this incredible park** in one of their jeeps because I'm really interested in dinosaurs. It would be so exciting to watch a Brachiosaourus eating leaves from the tall trees in the huge forests. Although, I wouldn't like to meet the really scary ones because they are carnivores!

7 Read the description again and answer the questions.

1 Match these headings to the paragraphs.
   a Description; **b** Location; **c** Opinion
2 Find examples in the text of adjectives used to describe the place and the animals.
3 Which expressions does the writer use to express his/her opinions? Find examples.

> **Writing tip**
>
> Use paragraphs
> Organise your essay into clear paragraphs: Location, Description, Opinion.

8 Write a description of your favourite fictional place.

Step 1: Make notes	Write a list of adjectives to describe this place and its features.
Step 2: Writing	• Remember to use paragraphs. • Check for correct punctuation and good use of adjectives. • Give your personal opinion.
Step 3: Read and check	Swap with a partner. Give your opinion. I'd love to visit this place too because…

> 3.5 The Lost City

We are going to...

- **read a story about *The Lost City*.**

1   Talk: Have you been on a journey? Tell your partner where you went, how you got there and what you did.

2   Look at the pictures of a journey. Who are the travellers? How do they get there? Why do you think they go on this journey?

 3   **Read and listen** to check your answers to Activity 2.

The Lost City

Yong-Hu and Ho-Shing walked through the valley. 'I'm getting tired,' Yong-Hu complained. 'Where are we going anyway?' he asked.

'We are going to find a city, a lost city. There are wondrous surprises that await the ones who find the ancient city.'

'Does anyone live there?' Yong-Hu asked.

'Not anymore. At one time it was the busiest city in all of China.'

'Why not?'

'Because it is too far out of the way for the trade routes.'

'What kinds of surprises are there? Good surprises?' Yong-Hu asked.

'Magical surprises,' Ho-Shing smiled. 'Come.'

'Is there bamboo in the lost city?' Yong-Hu asked.

'Much.'

'Good. Let's hurry up then. I'm starving.'

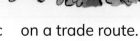

4   **Circle the correct answer.**

1   The Lost city is...
    a   in a remote location.   b   near the city.   c   on a trade route.

2   The city...
    a   is not a safe place.   b   has many surprises.   c   is very busy.

After several hours, Ho-Shing stopped. 'See the mountains ahead? We are nearly there. Another hour.'

Just then they heard a growling sound. 'What was that?' Yong-Hu asked.

'A tiger, but it isn't near us. Its roar is echoing off the tall mountains.'

'There it is! There is the lost city! We have found it at last,' Ho-Shing smiled.

'It is magnificent, Ho-Shing. The walls are high and the roofs of the buildings sparkle in the sunshine. Are they made of jade?' Yong-Hu asked.

'There is much green jade, ivory, gold, silver, and even red rubies. We must hurry,' Ho-Shing said.

'How do we get inside?' Yong-Hu wondered.

'We must climb these steps,' Ho-Shing said, pointing to very steep steps that led to the top of the wall.

Yong-Hu laughed and ran up the stairs. After he'd climbed twenty of them he stopped and took a few breaths. 'I think I'll walk slowly up the rest of them.'

3   Yong-Hu…
   a   ran up all the steps to the Lost City.
   b   couldn't climb to the top of the steps.
   c   ran up twenty stairs and then walked the rest.

'Ah, there is where we need to go,' he said to Yong-Hu as he reached the top step, 'over there, in the middle of the city.'

'That is where we shall find our surprises,' Ho-Shing said.

They climbed down the steps on the other side of the wall.

'We need to treat this place with respect. Be quiet. Don't touch anything until I say so,' he warned his friend.

When they reached the centre of town, a huge, golden gong hung from poles. Several Chinese statues of lions surrounded it. 'Look at their ruby eyes!' Yong-Hu said. 'Can I bang the gong?' he asked.

'Yes,' the wiser panda said.

Yong-Hu picked up the stick and hit the **gong**.

4 Where do the pandas need to go to find surprises?
  a They need to go down the steps.
  b They need to go to the statue with lions.
  c They need to go to the middle of the city.

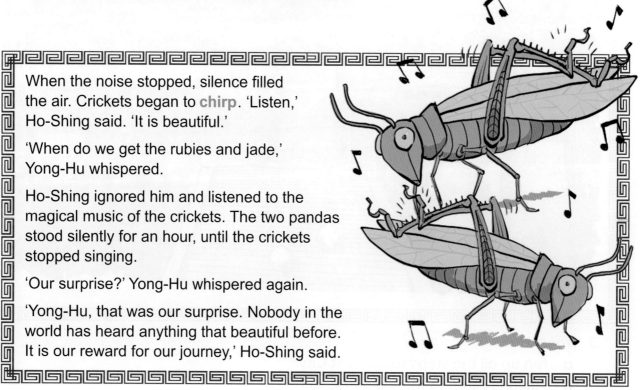

When the noise stopped, silence filled the air. Crickets began to **chirp**. 'Listen,' Ho-Shing said. 'It is beautiful.'

'When do we get the rubies and jade,' Yong-Hu whispered.

Ho-Shing ignored him and listened to the magical music of the crickets. The two pandas stood silently for an hour, until the crickets stopped singing.

'Our surprise?' Yong-Hu whispered again.

'Yong-Hu, that was our surprise. Nobody in the world has heard anything that beautiful before. It is our reward for our journey,' Ho-Shing said.

5 Yong-Hu's surprise was…
  a the bamboo.
  b the magical music of the crickets.
  c the rubies and jade.

> 'What about the jade? What about the gold, silver, rubies and ivory?'
> Yong-Hu asked.
>
> 'We cannot touch these things. They belong to the people who
> lived once in this lost city. You can eat all the bamboo you want,
> but the rest must stay within these walls,' Ho-Shing explained.
>
> At the mention of bamboo, Yong-Hu forgot about all the precious
> jewels and riches. 'Bamboo!' He ran off to search for his feast.
>
> *Margo Fallis*

5 Word study: **Match the words in blue in the text with the definitions below.**

  a The sound crickets and birds make.
  b A tall, leafy plant that pandas eat.
  c A red precious stone.
  d The sound a lion makes.
  e A green precious stone.
  f A large, circular instrument made of metal or gold.

6 **Find the past simple of these verbs in the text.**

| walk | hear | find | smile | forget | stand | run | climb | take | reach |

7 **Complete these sentences with a verb from Activity 6 in the past simple.**

  a They _____ a loud roar.
  b He _____ up the steps to the lost city.
  c Ho-shing smiled as he _____ the stairs.
  d When Yong-Hu saw the bamboo he _____ about the jewels.
  e The two pandas _____ in silence listening to the crickets singing.

8 **Values: Looking after our environment**

  a Why were there no people living in the city? Where have they gone?
  b Many people move from the country to the city to work, but this means the cities become dirtier and more crowded. Discuss ways in which we can make cities cleaner.

> 3.6 Project challenge

Project A: Design and draw your own fictional place

1 Before you design and draw your fictional place.
Draw a mind map with:

  a the name of your fictional place
  b adjectives to describe it
  c geographical or unusual features
  d animals or imaginary creatures or people.

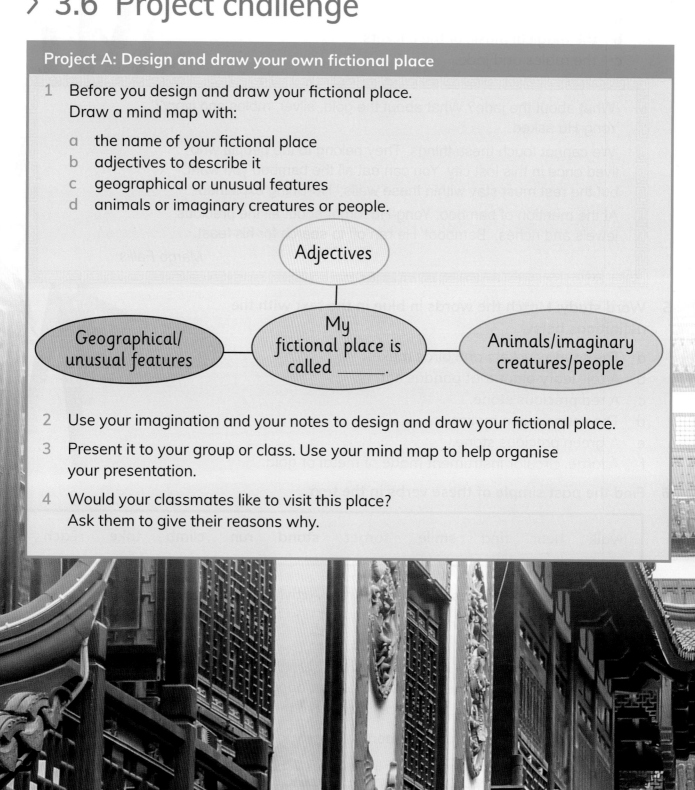

Adjectives

My
fictional place is
called _____.

Geographical/
unusual features

Animals/imaginary
creatures/people

2 Use your imagination and your notes to design and draw your fictional place.

3 Present it to your group or class. Use your mind map to help organise
your presentation.

4 Would your classmates like to visit this place?
Ask them to give their reasons why.

Project B: A city in the world

1 In groups, choose a continent (or your teacher will assign you one).

2 Select a country in this continent and find out which are the major cities.

3 Decide on which city you are going to write about in your group.
   Find information about your city online.
   Use these headings and make notes in each section.

> 1 Location:
>   • Geographical location (*It's in the north, east, south, west.*)
>   • Landscape (*It's mountainous. / It's on the coast. / It's in the country.*)
> 2 Size and population (*Shanghai is the most populated city in China. / It's bigger than New York.*)
> 3 Adjectives to describe the city (*It's a modern, noisy city with lots of traffic and people.*)
> 4 Interesting facts and places to visit. Think about historical landmarks, museums, famous shops or a sports stadium.

4 Use your notes to write a description about your city.

5 Find photos online or draw pictures to illustrate your group's description.
   Stick your photos and drawings around your description.
   Display on the classroom walls.

6 Walk around the classroom. Read other descriptions.
   Choose one you would like to visit. Give reasons why.

What did you enjoy most about this project?

> 3.7 What do you know now?

Where would be an ideal place to live?

1 Write down three adjectives to describe the city and the country.

4 Tell you partner about your favourite fictional place. Use adjectives from the unit to describe it.

2 Use the comparatives of your adjectives to write four sentences comparing the city and the country.

5 How many expressions can you think of to give an opinion?

3 Write two sentences about where you live using the superlative form.

6 Write sentences using these verbs in the past simple.

| ride | go | live |
| have | travel | work |

Look what I can do

Write or show examples in your notebook.

I can compare and talk about the city and the country.

I can draw a 3D optical illusion.

I can use the past simple to talk about places in the past.

I can write a description about a fictional place.

I can understand a story about *The Lost City*.

Check your progress 1

1   **Read the clues and guess the words.**

a   This adjective describes someone who studies hard.

b   This is when your head hurts.

c   This is something we walk over to cross a road safely.

d   This is good for your bones.

e   This adjective describes someone who talks a lot.

f   This is something which controls the traffic.

g   This helps your muscles to grow.

h   This is the opposite of outgoing.

i   This adjective means very big.

2   **Word race. Now add another similar word to match each sentence in Activity 1. You have five minutes!**

a talkative, outgoing

3   **Play noughts (0) and crosses (X). Work in pairs and follow the instructions.**

a   Choose nine words from Units 1–3 and write them in your grid.

b   Draw another blank nine square grid.

c   Take turns to choose a number. Your partner says the word for you to make a sentence with. If it's correct you can draw your nought 0 or cross X in the blank grid.

1 nervous	2	3
4	5	6
7	8	9

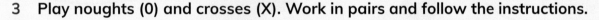

0	X	X
X	0	X
X	X	0

Ahmed is nervous because he has an English exam.

4 **Work in pairs. Each sentence has an error. Take turns to roll a dice and choose the sentence with the same number. Can you correct the errors?**

1   Wei is very excited in going on holiday.

2   She's very good of singing.

3   We should eat food with fewer salt.

4   You must to use a mosquito net when you sleep.

5   The country is more clean than the city.

6   When he was younger, my grandad ride his bike to work.

5 **Interview your partner. Write a question for each of the topics below.**

family   friends   favourite things   personality   sports   school

Have you got any brothers or sisters?

Yes, I've got one brother.

6 **Write a survey about towns and the country.**
Use the adjectives from the box.
Write three comparative questions and three superlative questions.

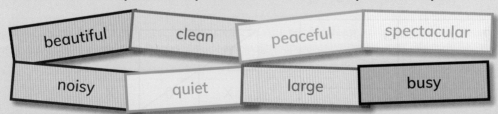

beautiful   clean   peaceful   spectacular   noisy   quiet   large   busy

Is it noisier in towns or in the country?

7 **Do the survey with a partner. Ask them to give a reason for their answers.**

It's noisier in towns because there is more traffic.

4 ▷ Special occasions

We are going to...

- **listen** to children from different cultures describing a celebration
- **learn about** time zones and how people celebrate New Year around the world
- **talk about** an important celebration in my culture
- **use** the present continuous to talk about future plans and arrangements
- **write** about a traditional food
- **enjoy and understand** an extract from Horrid Henry's birthday party.

Getting started

How are celebrations in your country similar or different to those in other countries?

a Look carefully at each of the photos. Write down three words to describe what you can see. Compare with a partner.
b How are they celebrating in the photos?
c Where are they celebrated? Do you have celebrations like this in your country?
d Which one looks the most interesting to you? Explain why.

Holi

A birthday party

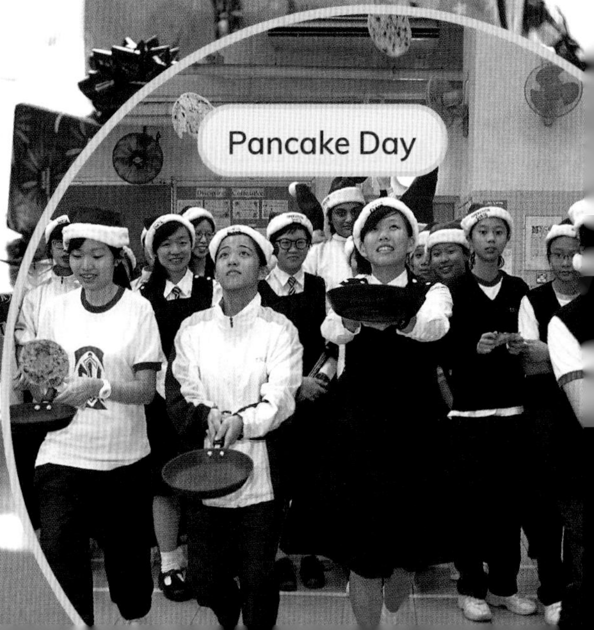

Pancake Day

Watch this!

> 4.1 What celebrations and holidays are important in your country?

We are going to...

- listen to children from different cultures describing celebrations.

1   **Talk: What was your last celebration? Write notes using the headings below.**

> Food or drink
>
> Sounds or music
>
> Smells
>
> Games or activities

2   **In pairs, describe your celebration from Activity 1. Can your partner guess what you were celebrating?**

We ate special food. We sang songs about...

3   **Vocabulary: How many of these words can you see in the photos below? Check any words you don't know in your dictionary.**

> fireworks   costumes   a feast
> **decorations**   lanterns   **lights**
> **paint**   parades   **symbols**   candles

4   **Listen to the sounds you can hear from the celebrations in the photos. Match them to photos a–c in Activity 3.**

I can hear a guitar and people singing. I think it's Spanish music. I think it's photo...

5 Listen to a girl describing one of the celebrations. Which photo is it? What does she like about it?

6 Listen again. Answer these questions.

    a What do they decorate their houses with?
    b How does she describe her street during the New Year celebrations?
    c What's the name of the special dance?
    d What materials are used to make the dragon?

7 Which celebration in the photos would you most like to go to? Why?

8 Listen to a description of two different festivals. Complete the notes below for each one.

- _____ is celebrated between / at _____.

- It lasts for _____.

- People decorate / have / go _____.

- The festival celebrates _____.

9 Talk: Use the vocabulary from Activity 3 and the phrases in Activity 8 to describe a festival or a celebration in your country.

〉 4.2 Problem solving

We are going to...

- **learn about time zones and discover how people celebrate New Year around the world.**

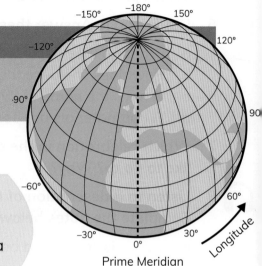

1 **Do the time quiz. Write true (T) or false (F).**

a There are 20 time zones around the world. _____

b The Earth turns 360° in 24 hours. _____

c If I fly east to west on a plane, it's later. _____

d If I fly west to east on a plane, it's earlier. _____

 2 **Read and listen to the article to find out the answers to the quiz.**

The Greenwich Meridian (Longitude zero degrees) in London is the starting point of every time zone. There are 24 time zones around the world.

The Earth is a sphere divided into 360° with longitude lines running from North to South. It turns 360° in 24 hours, so if you divide 360° by 24 you can work out how many degrees the Earth moves in one hour. The answer is 15° in one hour. These time zones make it easy for us to calculate the time anywhere in the world!

The International date line is halfway around the world from the Prime Meridian. It marks the change from one day to the next. If you travel from west to east you add a day and from east to west you subtract a day. Amazing but true!

Because of time zones, New Year's Eve is celebrated 24 times around the world! The first to celebrate are the people who live in Samoa and Kiribati and one of the last places to celebrate is Honolulu. Popular festivities are fireworks displays and parties, but there are some unusual traditions too. In Spain they eat 12 grapes, one for each strike of the clock at midnight, and the people who live in Greece hang an onion on the door. It's a symbol of a new start.

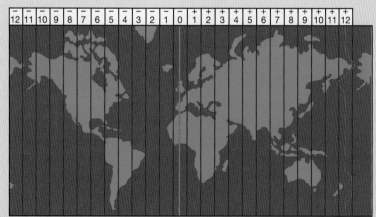

Greenwich Meridian   International Dateline

3 What time is it in these cities when you are celebrating New Year in your country? Use the information on the map to help you.

1   2   3

Berlin   Moscow   New York

Key words: Problem solving

divide: to separate into parts ÷

work out: to understand or solve something

subtract: to deduct/ remove a part or number from something −

add: to increase +

calculate: to work something out from figures

Use of English – Defining relative clauses

Defining relative clauses give us important information about people, places and things and explain why this information is important. Examples of these are **who**, **which**, **that** and **where**.

We use **who** or **that** to talk about people.

The boy **who** is singing is my friend.

We use **that** or **which** to talk about things.

Grapes are the fruit **which** the Spanish eat at midnight.

We use **where** to talk about places.

Sydney is the place **where** you can see the best fireworks.

4 Use of English: Fill in the gaps with the correct defining clause.

 a The first people to celebrate are the people _____ live in Samoa and Kiribati.
 b The people _____ live in Greece hang an onion on the door.
 c Honolulu is _____ the last New Year's celebrations take place.
 d I like parties _____ have fireworks.

5 Talk: How are New Year celebrations in your country similar or different to those in Spain and Greece?

6 Complete the notes about your New Year celebration. Share with your class.

I'm going to celebrate New Year's Eve in…
We're going to watch / sing / eat…

〉 4.3 Personal celebrations

We are going to...

- talk about a celebration which is important in our culture
- use the present continuous to talk about future plans and arrangements.

1 **Talk: Do you celebrate a special age in your country? What sort of celebration do you have?**

2 **Listen: to children from different cultures talking about 'coming of age' celebrations.**
Are any of the celebrations similar to the ones celebrated in your culture?

Listening tip

Making connections

We make connections when we compare the information we hear with our own lives and culture.

3 **Listen again. Match the photos to the speakers.**

A

Speaker 1

B

Speaker 2

C

Speaker 3

4 **Listen again. Copy the table into your notebook and complete it.**

Country	A tradition	Age	Special clothes	A feast/special food
Japan				
	Quinceanera			
		21	None	

5 **Word study: Match the verbs to the nouns. You can use some words more than once.**

(eat) (receive) (make) (a song) (a candle) (cake)

(light) (get) (sing) (a blessing) (food) (a gift)

6 **Pronunciation: Listen and repeat. How are the words connected?**

a sing ⌢ a song

b get ⌢ a gift

c light ⌢ a candle

7 **Use of English: Complete the sentences with the correct verbs and the present continuous.**

> **Use of English – Present continuous with future meaning**
>
> We use the present continuous to talk about plans and arrangements that have already been made. The contracted form is more common.
>
> **I'm** (am) **getting** my first kimono this Friday.
> **She's** (is) **having** a birthday party on Saturday.

| bring | plan | have | **arrive** | travel |

a The guests _____ at 6 p.m.

b We _____ lots of party games for tonight.

c He _____ (not) _____ my present to the party later.

d They _____ by car to my party on Saturday.

e I _____ a sleepover after the party

> **Speaking tip**
>
> Make it personal
>
> Use information about your own life to make your presentation more personal.

8 **Present it! My coming of age celebration**

- Research facts about your celebration. Ask your parents and your grandparents when it takes place.
- Make notes about the celebration – traditions, costumes, ceremonies, symbols and food.
- Imagine that the celebration is very soon. Use the present continuous to express what is already planned for the celebration.
- Give your opinion on this celebration. Is it important to you? Why? If not, who is it important for?

❯ 4.4 A traditional food

We are going to...

- write about a traditional food.

1 **Talk: Work in pairs and talk about the questions.**

    a Do you eat special food on certain days of the year?

    b Do you make or buy the food for this special celebration?

    c What does it taste like? Do you like it?

2 **Read about these traditional foods. Would you like to try them? Why? Why not?**

Mid-Autumn festival

`a tradition`

Mid-Autumn festival is celebrated in China every year on the 15th day of the 8th month of the Chinese lunar calendar. It is also called the Moon Festival. It marks the celebration of the harvest. **People present moon cakes to their friends and families** to wish them a long and happy life. The moon cakes are **made of pastry and filled with** <u>sweet</u> or <u>salty</u> **fillings such as fruit or beans**.

Bánh Chung   `interesting adjectives`

The Tet festival is celebrated every year in Vietnam. It marks the arrival of spring and takes place on the same day as the Chinese New Year celebrations. Tet is a time for family parties and feasts. Bánh Chung which **is made of** <u>sticky rice</u> **and** <u>meat</u> **or a** <u>bean filling</u> are usually prepared and eaten during this festival. They are wrapped in banana leaves and boiled for 12 hours! They are soft, chewy and sweet!

`ingredients`

3 Answer the questions and complete the table with information from the texts.

	Mid-Autumn festival	Bánh Chung
1 Where are the festivals celebrated?		In Vietnam
2 What do they mark?	Celebration of the harvest	
3 What is the traditional food made of?		
4 What does it taste like?		Soft...

4 Write about a celebration in your culture. Follow the steps below to help you.

Step 1: Planning	• Choose your favourite celebration or festival. • Make notes about the questions in Activity 3. • Give a personal opinion about the celebration and the food.
Step 2: Writing	Use this useful language in your description: It is celebrated in (the Spring / January) It marks (the end of / beginning of / the arrival of) It's made of / with... It tastes... (choose interesting adjectives to describe food)
Step 3: Read and check	Swap with your partner. Give your opinion about the festival and the food. (I love Eid cookies too!)

5 Now you have finished your description, check that you have included everything on the checklist.

Checklist ✓	
Useful language	☐
Interesting adjectives	☐
Write a fact	☐
Write an opinion	☐

6 Present, display or publish your work.

⟩ 4.5 Horrid Henry's Birthday Party

We are going to...

- **read an extract from *Horrid Henry's Birthday Party*.**

1 Do you invite friends to your house?
When do you invite them? What do you do?

25 2 Read and listen to the text.
What is Horrid Henry organising?

Horrid Henry's Birthday Party

Horrid Henry sat in his fort holding a pad of paper.
On the front cover in big capital letters Henry wrote:

HENRY'S PARTY PLANS TOP SECRET!!!

At the top of the first page Henry had written:

Guests

A long list followed. Then Henry stared at the names and chewed his pencil. Actually, I don't want Margaret, thought Henry. Too moody. He crossed out Moody Margaret's name.

And I definitely don't want Susan. Too crabby.

In fact, I don't want any girls at all, thought Henry.

He crossed out Clever Clare. And Lazy Linda.

Then there was Anxious Andrew. Nope, thought Henry, crossing him off. He's no fun.

Toby was possible, but Henry didn't really like him. Out went Tough Toby.

William? No way, thought Henry. He'll be crying the second he gets zapped. Out went Weepy William.

Ralph? Henry considered. Ralph would be good because he was sure to get into trouble. On the other hand, he hadn't invited Henry to his party. Rude Ralph was struck off.

So were Babbling Bob, Jolly Josh, Greedy Graham and Dizzy Dave.

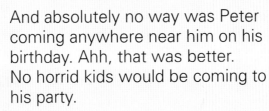

And absolutely no way was Peter coming anywhere near him on his birthday. Ahh, that was better. No horrid kids would be coming to his party.

There was only one problem. Every single name was crossed off. No guests meant no presents.

Francesca Simon

3 Listen and read again. Answer the questions.

a How many guests does Henry have on his list to begin with?

b Who are the first four guests he crosses out on his list?

c Does he want to invite girls to his party?

d Why does he cross Anxious Andrew off his list?

e Why does he cross Ralph off his list?

f Who do you think Peter is?

g What is the problem in the end?

h How do you think Henry feels about this problem?

4 Word study: Match the adjectives to the definitions. Use your dictionary to help you.

1	clever	a	strong
2	moody	b	someone who cries a lot
3	jolly	c	intelligent
4	tough	d	not polite
5	lazy	e	bad-tempered
6	anxious	f	good-humoured
7	weepy	g	not hardworking
8	rude	h	worried/nervous

5 Match the opposites. Use your dictionary to help you.

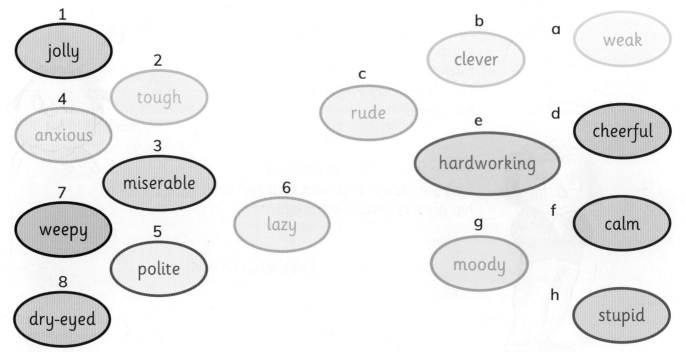

1 jolly
2 tough
4 anxious
3 miserable
7 weepy
5 polite
8 dry-eyed
6 lazy

a weak
b clever
c rude
d cheerful
e hardworking
f calm
g moody
h stupid

6 **Who's on the guest list? Match the descriptive clues to the children.**

1 He's always smiling and laughing.	a Moody Margaret
2 She always gets top marks in exams.	b Rude Ralph
3 He doesn't speak nicely to anyone.	c Clever Clare
4 One minute she's happy, then she's angry.	d Lazy Linda
5 He's so emotional!	e Weepy William
6 She never hands in her homework on time.	f Jolly Josh

7 **Values: Which positive adjectives would you use to describe your friends? In pairs talk about each other's positive characteristics. Give examples.**

You're cheerful and you always try to make me happy.

Do you have any negative aspects that you think you can improve?

 8 **Pronunciation: Listen to the pronunciation of the 'ough' words. Use coloured pens to circle the words which sound the same. There are three different sounds.**

1 **tough**

2 en**ough**

3 b**ought**

4 d**ough**

5 r**ough**

6 th**ough**

7 th**ough**t

9 **Write a guest list for your birthday. Explain why you want to invite each person. Use positive adjectives to describe each person.**

I'm going to invite Happy Hassan because he will make the party fun.

10 **Plan a party with a friend. Think about the questions below.**

a Is there a theme to the party? (fancy dress, a disco)

b What food will you need?

c What games will you play?

d How long will it last?

e Make a poster to advertise your party. Put the posters up around your classroom – which party would you like to go to? Why?

› 4.6 Project challenge

Project A: Find out about and play a New Year party game

1   Research these traditional New Year games played in Greece and Romania.

Vasilias folk game (Greece)

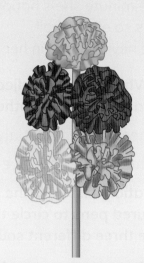

Sorcova (Romania)

2   Find out how to play these games. Make notes.

3   Tell another group how to play the game.

4   Give step-by-step instructions using these words:

first	then	next	after	finally

5   Have a class vote on which game you like best and play it in class.

Project B: Design a poster for a special occasion in your school

1 Look at the poster some children have made for a celebration.

   a What's the name of the celebration?
   b What day is it celebrated on?
   c What are they going to wear?
   d What are they going to do?

2 In pairs, design a poster for a celebration at your school.

Step 1: Decide in your group which celebration you are going to design the poster for (if possible it should be a real celebration that is going to take place at your school).

Step 2: Create a slogan. 'If you love bright colours and music, then don't miss our Diwali party!'

Step 3: Include general information: When, Where, What games and activities, What time, clothes.

Step 4: Draw a picture to illustrate the poster or cut out pictures from magazines.

Step 5: Stick your posters around the school to advertise the celebration.

3 Work with a new pair. Tell them about your celebration.

Your classmates will use the checklist to evaluate your project.

> # Flying pancakes! Join in the race!
>
> 16th February in the playground at 12.30 p.m.
>
> Bring a chef's hat and a frying pan!
>
> Tossing the pancake race.

How well did you communicate with your group on the project? What might you do differently next time?

> 4.7 What do you know now?

How are celebrations in your country similar or different to those in others?

1 Write a list of five words that are connected to celebrations.

4 Name all the festivals and celebrations you have learned about in this unit. Select your favourite ones and compare with your partner.

2 Choose three words from your list in number 1 and describe them for your partner to guess.

5 Use defining clauses to describe the following:
  a *Bánh Chung is a...*   c *A lantern is a...*
  b *Tossing the pancake is a ...*   d *A quinceañera is a...*

3 Tell your partner how you celebrate New Year with your family.

6 Write the coming of age celebrations in your culture on a time line.
0 years _____ **100 years**

7 Work out what time it is in Australia and Canada now.

Look what I can do

Write or show examples in your notebook.

	😐	🙂
I can compare and talk about how I celebrate special occasions.	○	○
I can read and understand a text about time zones and how people celebrate New Year around the world.	○	○
I can talk about an important celebration in my culture.	○	○
I can use the present continuous to talk about future plans and arrangements.	○	○
I can write about a traditional food.	○	○
I can enjoy and understand an extract from *Horrid Henry's Birthday Party*.	○	○

5 ▶ Our brains

We are going to...

- **do** memory and brain experiments
- **discover** interesting facts about our brains
- **use** the zero conditional to talk about the body's involuntary actions
- **discuss** what's good for the brain and how we should protect it
- **write** a scientific report about an experiment
- **read a poem** *The girl who thought in pictures.*

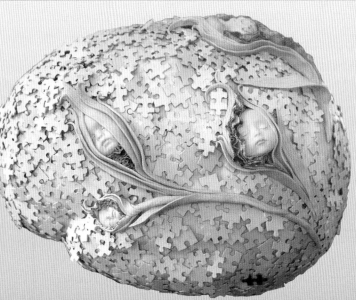

Getting started

What's amazing about our brains?

a Look carefully at each of the sculptures. What can you see in each one?
b What do you think the artist's message is about the brain? Discuss as a group.
c Which one do you like best? Give reasons why.

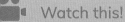 Watch this!

❯ 5.1 Do you have a good memory?

We are going to...

- **do** memory and brain experiments.

1 **Talk: How good is your memory? Work in pairs and talk about the questions.**

   a   What did you have for breakfast this morning?
   b   What was your favourite toy when you were four years old?
   c   What were you doing 30 minutes ago?
   d   What is the first holiday you can remember? What was special about it?
   e   What did we do in our last English class?
   f   Can you remember one of the presents your parents bought you when you were little?

2 **Which questions in Activity 1 are about short-term memory and which ones are about long-term memory? Then read the solution to find out.**

If you could answer questions a, c and e then you have a super cool, short-term memory! If you couldn't answer any then you need to improve it!	If you could answer questions b, d and f then you have an excellent long-term memory! If you could answer two, then it's not too bad, but you need to exercise your brain more!

3 **Vocabulary: What's happening?**
   Match the words and expressions to the actions.

yawning	hitting a knee reflex	**pulling away from something hot**
sneezing	a beating heart	pulling away from something sharp

a   b   c

d   e   f

4 **Talk: When your body does these actions, do you have to think to make them happen?**

5 **Listen** and tick the actions the scientist talks about in Activity 4.

 6 **Listen** again and complete the sentences below.

> **Use of English – Zero conditional**
>
> If you **do** exercise, your heart **beats** faster
> If you **touch** something hot, you **pull** your hand away fast
> When you **yawn**, your friend **yawns** too!

a If you touch something hot, neurons send information to your brain at _____.

b A sneeze travels very fast at about _____.

c The average heartbeat of a _____ year-old is _____ beats per minute.

7 **Use of English: Match the parts of the sentences to form true sentences using the zero conditional.**

1 When I'm excited or nervous about something...
2 If I tread on a sharp object...
3 If a doctor hits my knee reflex...

a it springs up!
b my heart beats faster.
c I pull away my foot fast!

8 **Read** the instructions and try these experiments with a partner.

Experiment 1:

Student A: Hold a ruler just above your partner's open thumb and first finger. Count to three and drop the ruler. Swap roles.

Student B: How fast are your reflexes? Hold your hand just under the ruler. Catch it between your thumb and finger as quickly as possible. How fast were you? Swap roles.

Experiment 2:

Do you have good short-term memory? Try this experiment. Put 8–10 objects under a cloth or a piece of paper. Show your partner the objects for 30 seconds then cover them up again. How many can your partner remember? Take turns.

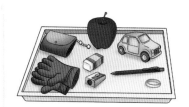

Experiment 3:

Find your pulse in your wrist or neck. Close your eyes and count the number of beats for 30 seconds. Your teacher will tell you when to stop. Now multiply the number of beats by two to get your heartbeats per minute. Is yours similar to your partner's?

> 5.2 The amazing human brain

We are going to...

- discover interesting facts about our brains.

1 **Talk:** What does the human brain look like? How big do you think it is?

2 **Draw** a life-size picture of the brain.

3 **Read** this description about the size and colour of the brain. Compare these measurements to your own drawing. How accurate were you?

> The Human brain is a wrinkly, grey organ, the size of two fists put together. It weighs 1.3 kg. It's 16 cm long, 14 cm wide and 10 cm deep. It controls everything we do from learning, breathing and feeling emotions. It uses 20% of all your energy and stops growing when you are about 20.

fists

 4 **Read and listen** to the text. Number the parts of the brain.

| brain stem | cerebrum | cerebellum |

The brain is like the body's computer because it controls everything we do. The brain has three main parts:

The cerebrum, which is the biggest part of the brain, has a left and right side. The left side is usually better at problem solving and maths. It also controls your speech. The right side is more creative and helps us to understand music, colours, shapes and art.

The cerebellum is located at the back of the brain and is much smaller than the cerebrum. It controls your balance, **movement** and coordination.

The brain stem connects the rest of the brain to the spinal cord, which runs down your neck and back. It controls the body's functions such as **breathing**, **digestion** and **blood circulation**. It's like the brain's secretary because it sorts through all the messages sent from the 100 billion tiny cells called neurons located throughout the body. They send information from your body to your brain and back again at an incredible 240 km per hour – just like a high-speed train!

5 Read the text again. Pay special attention to the information about the different parts of the brain and their functions. Copy and fill in the mind maps.

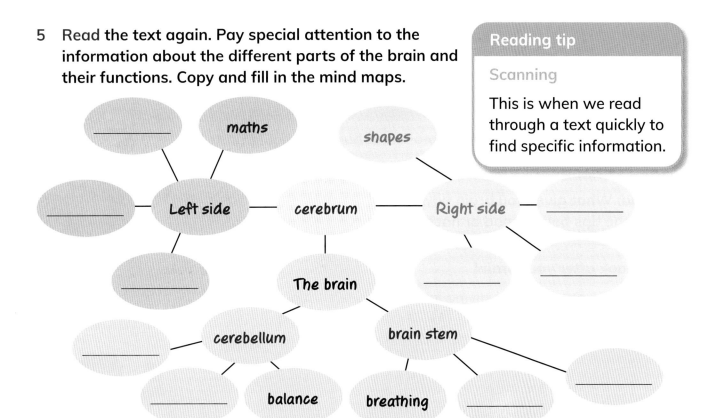

Use of English – Tag questions

We use tag questions when we think we know the answer, but we need confirmation.

We add a negative tag to a positive sentence and a positive tag to a negative sentence.

The brain **is** 14 cm wide, **isn't it?**

The left part of the brain **controls** speech, **doesn't it?**

Scientists **don't know** everything about the brain, **do they?**

Key words: Body functions

breathing: how the body takes in oxygen and expels carbon dioxide from our lungs
movement: how we move from one place to another
digestion: how the body turns food into energy for us to use
blood circulation: how blood carries materials such as oxygen and nutrients around our body

6 Use of English: Test your understanding of these numbers in the text. Take turns. Cover the text and confirm the answer with your partner.

20% is the amount of energy the brain uses, isn't it?

| 100 billion | 1.3 kg | 20 | **16 cm** | 240 km per hour | **10 cm** |

81 >

› 5.3 Brain power!

We are going to...

- discuss what's good for our brain and how we should protect it.

1   Read: **What gives you brain power?**
    Are the tips below good or not?

> **Look after your brain!**
>
> - Be careful when diving into a swimming pool or the sea because it can be dangerous for your brain.
> - Juggling can make your brain stronger!
> - Pizza and cookies are excellent forms of brain food!
> - Fish like salmon is very good for your brain because it contains Omega-3, which helps build brain and nerve cells.
> - You should wear a helmet when you ride your bike, but it isn't necessary on a scooter.
> - Playing music is good for the brain.

🎧 29   2   **Listen to two children discussing the quotes about brain power. Are their opinions similar to yours?**

🎧 29   3   **Listen again. Which of these expressions do they use to express and share opinions?**

> What's your opinion about...?   I definitely agree
>
> I share your view on that   **Building on (Ahmed's) point...**
>
> **I think you're right**   **I totally agree**   **I think I disagree**
>
> What's your view on...?   I definitely disagree!
>
> **I absolutely agree with you!**

4 **Pronunciation: Listen and repeat these expressions. Listen to the word stress and try to be emphatic!**

> I absolûtely disagree!

> I tôtally agree with you!

> I dėfinitely think you're right!

5 **Give your opinion about the tips in Activity 1. Follow your teacher's instructions to do the activity.**

- Remember to use the useful expressions in Activities 3 and 4.
- Use adverbs to be emphatic!

6 **Read the scientific advice about what's good and bad for your brain. Were your opinions correct? Does anything surprise you?**

> **Speaking tip**
>
> Be emphatic!
>
> When you want to make a strong point, you can use adverbs like *definitely*, *absolutely* and *totally* before the verb
>
> I **definitely** agree with you!

1 When diving into a pool you should always check the depth before you do so. Either ask your parents or a pool attendant if you aren't sure. Diving into the sea can be very dangerous because there are often rocks that you can't see. If you hit you head, you could seriously injure your brain.

2 Pizza and fries are not the best brain food. Eat more fresh fruit and vegetables, nuts and fatty fish if you want your brain to be in top condition!

3 Salmon is excellent brain food because it contains Omega-3s.

4 Start juggling! New evidence shows it could improve connections in your brain.

5 Always protect your head when on a scooter, bike, skateboard or motorbike. If you damage your brain, it can't always be repaired like a broken bone.

6 Playing a musical instrument can improve your memory, coordination and even your reading skills!

7 **Talk: Choose two things you could do to improve your brain power. Compare with your partner.**

83 〉

❭ 5.4 A report for a science investigation

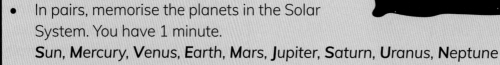

We are going to...

- write a report about a science investigation.

1 **Talk: Are you good at remembering lists of words and numbers? Try this memory experiment.**

- In pairs, memorise the planets in the Solar System. You have 1 minute.
  Sun, Mercury, Venus, Earth, Mars, Jupiter, Saturn, Uranus, Neptune
- Now cover the list. Take turns to say them in the correct order.
- Try the memory test again. Make a silly sentence with words that start with the first letter of each planet. For example: Sam my very elegant monkey just served us noodles.

2 **Did you remember the order of the planets better?**

3 **Read Mia's report about her science investigation into memory.**

Name: Mia

Project title: The planets in the Solar System   reporting language

Objective: To find out the best way to remember the order of the planets in the Solar System through two experiments.

Materials: Pictures of the planets in the Solar System, pen, notebook

clear stages

Stages:

1 **First** we put the pictures in order and tried to memorise the order of the planets.

2 **Then** we invented a silly sentence to help us remember the order.

Results: reporting language

1 **We discovered that** learning the order with pictures was very helpful. 70% of the class got it right.

2 Using a sentence to remember the order of the planets was very successful. Everyone in the class got it right!

an opinion

Conclusion: To conclude, in my opinion, the best way to remember the order of the planets is to make up a silly sentence with words that have the first letter of each planet.

4 Write: **You are going to do memory experiments with your group and write a report with your results.**

This memory test is about remembering words in English. It's to investigate how we can help our memory remember words better.

> **Writing tip**
>
> Reporting language
>
> ...to find out...   First, then, finally...
> We discovered   To conclude...
> that...   In my opinion,...

Step 1: Planning	Work in groups of four. Look at the vocabulary in Units 1, 2 and 3 and write five words for each of these categories on strips of paper: *Adjectives of personality, Common illnesses* and *Town and country words.*
Step 2: Experiment 1	• Mix up all the words and place them face up. • Take turns to look at them for two minutes – try to remember them all. • Turn the strips over. • How many can you remember? Write down the results. • Repeat with all your classmates.
Step 3: Experiment 2	• Group all the words into their categories before trying to remember them. • Take turns to look at them for two minutes. • Turn the strips over. • How many can you remember? Write down the results.
Step 4: Write a report	Write up a report about this memory experiment using Mia's model to help you. Which was the most successful? Give your opinion why.

⟩ 5.5 The girl who thought in pictures

We are going to...

- **read a poem *The girl who thought in pictures*.**

1 Talk: What do you understand from the title of this book?
   What do you think it's going to be about? Talk with a partner.

 2 Read and listen to Part 1 of the poem. Check your ideas from Activity 1.

The girl who thought in pictures

If you've ever felt different,
2 If you've ever felt low.
   If you don't quite fit in,
4 There's a name you should know
   Temple Grandin's that name,
6 **Unique** from the start
   An **unusual** girl,
8 She loved spinning circles
   And watching things **twirl**.
10 But some things she hated,
   Like certain loud sounds,

12 Or bright, **crowded** places—
   Large cities and towns.
14 **Frilly** dresses with **tags**
   Made her **itch**, pull and tug...
16 Something else that she hated?
   A BIG SQUEEZY **HUG**!

a

Glossary

twirl: turn around quickly
frilly: decorative material on a dress or skirt
itch: rub or scratch your skin with your nails

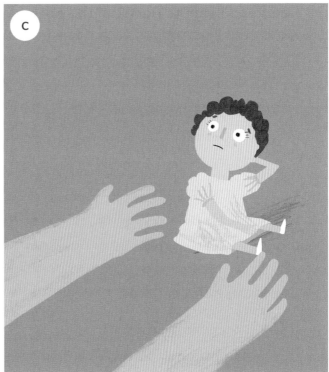

3 Read the poem again and match the illustrations a–c with a line in the poem.

4 Are these sentences true or false about Temple?

a She's different from other children.
b She loves spinning.
c She doesn't like busy places.
d She likes frilly dresses.
e She doesn't like cuddles.

5 Word study: Match the words in blue in the poem with these definitions.

a small labels on clothing
b a lot of people in one place
c one of a kind
d different
e to embrace someone

6 Talk: What makes Temple unique?
Do you think Part 1 of the poem has a positive message? Talk with a partner.

7 Read and listen to Part 2 of the poem.
Match the illustrations with a line in the poem.

A shy loner, this Temple,
2 But when she got mad,
When her feelings of stress
4 And frustration got bad,
Quite a **tantrum** she'd throw,
6 Kick, holler, bang, **shriek**
Yet still by age three,
8 Not one word did she speak.

'She'll never be normal,'
10 Was what some did say.
'Her brain's not quite right.
12 You must send her away.'
'AWAY? Not my Temple!'
14 Her mother proclaimed.
'We will figure this out.
16 You should all be ashamed!'

Then little, by little,
18 Though sometimes she **balked**,
Special teachers helped Temple,
20 And one day she talked!
And that thing with her brain...
22 It was Autism, see?
She was different, not less,
24 They all finally agreed.

d

e

Glossary

tantrum: when a young child gets angry
shriek: a loud, high cry
balk: protest (because you don't want to do something)

8 **Read Part 2 again and answer the questions.**

a What's different about Temple?

b Why does her mother get angry?

c Who helped Temple?

d What does everyone finally agree?

9 **Listen again. Can you find words in the poem that rhyme with the words below?**

mad	speak	say	proclaimed	talked	see

10 Vocabulary: Use these action verbs from the poem to complete these sentences.

itch	shriek	bang	hug	talked	twirl

a She _____ when she saw the spider.

b He always _____ his teddy bear at night.

c He _____ on the door, but no one let him in.

d The dancer _____ around the stage.

e Her woolly jumper made her _____.

11 Values: Being inclusive

a What is the message in this poem? How do you feel about it?

b Do you think everyone is different in some way?

c Why is it important to be fair to others?

d Do you treat everyone fairly and equally?

5.6 Project challenge

Project A: Make a brain comic

1. You're going to make a group brain comic about the most amazing things you've learned about the brain in this unit.

2. In groups, look back over the unit and choose the fact that most surprised or interested you. Compare opinions with your partners.

   The most interesting fact I've learned is...

3. Look at this brain comic below. Can you write the captions?

4. Now make your own group brain comic.
   Each person in the group writes a caption and draws a picture.

5. Stick them all together to form your comic and display in class.

Project B: Design a brain

1 Imagine you are taking part in a contest to draw, paint or make your very own interpretation of the brain.

2 Look back at the photos you discussed on page 77.

3 Think about what the brain means to you. Answers these questions.

   Is it the body's home? Is it a puzzle? Is it your computer system?

4 Design, draw and/or paint your entry to the contest.

5 Give it a title or write a short description explaining your artwork.

6 Display your art around the school for other children to see.

What do you like most about your project? Is there anything you would like to improve?

> 5.7 What do you know now?

What's amazing about our brains?

  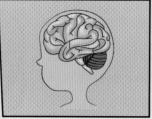 

1 Mime two involuntary actions for your partner to guess.

4 What does the Cerebellum control?

5 Ask your partner three questions using question tags.

2 Complete these sentences using the zero conditional.
When I'm excited...
If I touch something hot...

6 Name two things Temple loved as a girl and two things she hated.

3 Describe the Cerebrum to your partner.

7 Choose two facts that really interest you about the brain. Ask your partner if he/she agrees with you.

Look what I can do

Write or show examples in your notebook.

I can understand and do memory and brain experiments.

I can understand a scientist talking about the brain's functions.

I can use the zero conditional to talk about how my body works.

I can discuss what's good for the brain and how we should protect it.

I can write a scientific report about an experiment.

I can read a poem about a girl who is different.

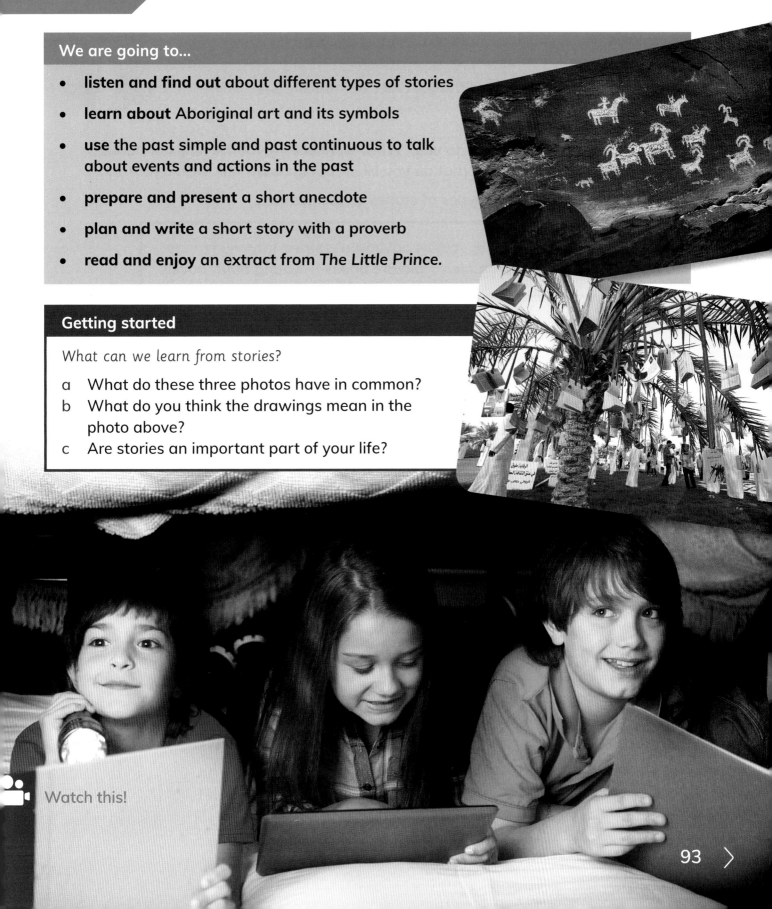

6 ▷ Great stories

We are going to...

- **listen and find out** about different types of stories
- **learn about** Aboriginal art and its symbols
- **use** the past simple and past continuous to talk about events and actions in the past
- **prepare and present** a short anecdote
- **plan and write** a short story with a proverb
- **read and enjoy** an extract from *The Little Prince.*

Getting started

What can we learn from stories?

a   What do these three photos have in common?
b   What do you think the drawings mean in the photo above?
c   Are stories an important part of your life?

Watch this!

〉 6.1 What's in a story?

We are going to...

- talk and find out about different types of stories.

1 Talk: What do stories mean to you? What were your favourite kinds of books when you were younger? What do you like reading now? Talk with a partner.

2 Vocabulary: Match these types of stories to the pictures.

> board books   comic adventure stories   family stories
> **fairy tales   fables   picture books   young adult novels**

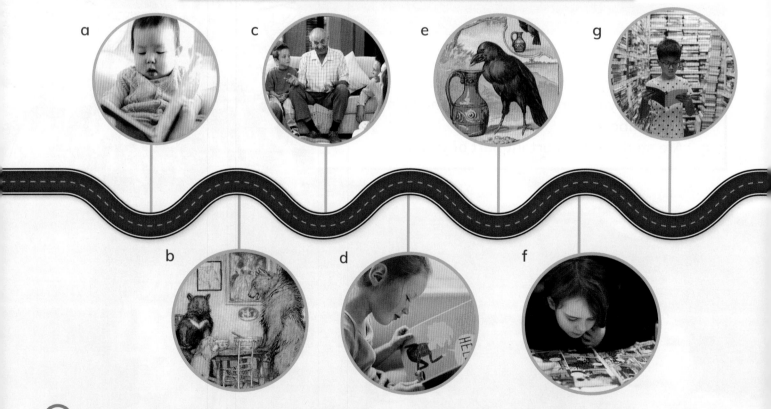

3 Listen to Banyu talking about the story experiences he has had.
Take notes. Did he like similar stories to you?
What do you have in common with him? Tell a partner.

I really like Aesop's fables too! My favourite is...

4 Listen to a storyteller reading extracts from two of the types of stories in Activity 3. What types of stories are they?

 5 Listen to Extract 2 again and write the missing words. What types of words are they?

Listening tip

Recognising context

Listen for clues in the text about the setting, the characters and the storyline to help identify the story type.

The Book Thief

The Cool detective gang were busy investigating in the woods _____¹ they heard something strange. 'SShhh!' said Lily. Dan _____² Sara stood still. The sound was coming from the big, ancient house. They moved closer and hid behind some trees, _____³ they couldn't see anything. _____⁴ a few minutes, they heard the sound of glass breaking, _____⁵ they moved nearer to where the sound came from. _____⁶ they saw a tiny figure jumping through a broken window into the library of the ancient house. Lily took out her binoculars, she could see the figure dressed in jeans and a blue sweatshirt throwing the books off the bookshelves; paperbacks, hardbacks, journals and diaries all fell to the floor. Pages fluttered in the air. The figure had to be looking for something…but what?

6 Use of English: Read the text again and match the uses to the correct connectives.

1 adding ideas
2 time or sequence
3 contrast ideas
4 results

a so
b and
c next
d but

Use of English – Connectives

Words like *and*, *after*, *but*, *so*, *when* and *next* are used to begin or connect parts of a sentence.

95

> 6.2 Aboriginal symbols and stories

We are going to...

- learn about Aboriginal art and its symbols.

Listening tip

Reading for gist

Read quickly through a text in order to answer a general question, decide on a topic, the type of text or the writer's feelings or opinions.

1 **Talk: What can you see in the artwork below? What's interesting about it?**

2 **Read and listen: What is Aboriginal art? How do they create it? Read and listen to the text.**

This is Aboriginal art made by the native people of Australia. Historians think that the Aboriginal people have lived in Australia for about 125 000 years and the oldest artwork ever found is about 40 000 years old. They painted on rocks and **bark** and carved sculptures too.

Dot painting is a popular form of Aboriginal art. The Aboriginal people used natural resources from the land such as ochre and **clay** to produce colours like white, yellow and red and they made black from **charcoal**. Yellow dots represented the sun and brown the **soil**. Red was used for the red, desert sand and white for the clouds and the sky. Dot paintings can be found on rocks and in caves and is now a very popular form of abstract art.

People believe they used dots to hide secret messages and information from the Europeans when they arrived in Australia. They also used circles, lines and symbols in their art too.

This type of art was often used to tell a story, to educate children about animals and nature and to pass on traditions and ideas about life.

Key words: Materials used in art

bark: the outer part of a tree
clay: a material from the earth which is soft when it's wet and hard when it's dry. We make cups and plates from it.
charcoal: a blackish material we use for barbecuing food
soil: the top layer of the earth where plants grow

3 **Re-read and listen again to the text and answer the questions.**

1 What do these colours represent in traditional dot paintings?

a ◯   b ◯   c ●   d ●

2 Why did they use dots?
3 What did they use this type of art for?
4 Do you like it? Explain why or why not.

4 **Talk: What symbols can you see in the dot painting in Activity 1?**
Do you think it tells a story?

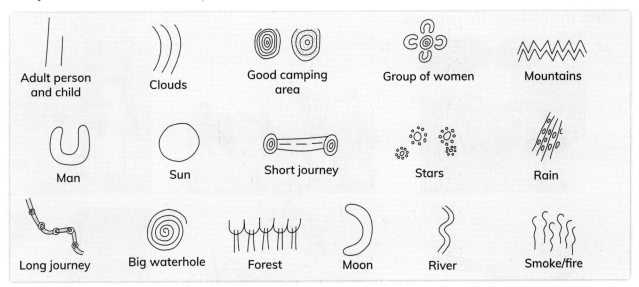

Adult person and child	Clouds	Good camping area	Group of women	Mountains
Man	Sun	Short journey	Stars	Rain
Long journey	Big waterhole	Forest	Moon	River	Smoke/fire

5 **Complete this short text with the correct word.** HW.
Use the symbols in Activity 4 to help you.

))) ¹ Clouds covered the sky and I could see ² _____ over

the ³ _____ . It was only a ⁴ _____ to reach

the ⁵ _____ . I ran through the ⁶ _____ and came to

a ⁷ _____ . I was thirsty. I smelt ⁸ _____ so I knew I was nearly there.

Then I saw a ⁹ _____ sitting around a ¹⁰ _____ .

6 **Write some sentences using these symbols.**
Give them to your partner to read and decode.

> 6.3 Telling an anecdote

We are going to...

- prepare and present a short anecdote about something which happened in our lives.

1   Talk: An anecdote is a short story about a real person or an event you have experienced. What's this anecdote about? Use the pictures to help you.

a

b

c

d

e

f

 2   Listen to Sofia's anecdote and check your ideas.

3   Match each sentence to the picture it describes.

1   Last year I went camping with my family in the mountains. ____c____
2   One day, we were hiking in the mountains. _____
3   They ran so fast and then they flapped their incredible wings to fly up into the sky. _____
4   We went rock climbing and we visited picturesque villages. _____
5   We hid in some bushes and there they were feeding and fighting. _____
6   We stopped and moved quietly towards the strange sound. _____

4   Talk: How did Sofia feel about the experience?

Use of English – Past simple and past continuous

We **were hiking** in the mountains **when** we **heard** a strange, loud noise.
As we **were looking** for somewhere to hide, we **heard** the noise again.

1 Which verbs are in the past continuous? Which verb is in the past simple?

2 Which verbs tell us about an action in progress?
Which verb tells us about an action that interrupts the first?

3 Which words can we use to link the two parts of the sentence?

5 **Listen again and tick the expressions you hear in the anecdote.**

I'll never forget the day when…

Suddenly…!

You'll never guess what we saw!

What happened next was…

6 Pronunciation: **Listen and practise the pronunciation of the expressions in Activity 5. We can use them to create excitement, or to express surprise or a sense of fear in a conversation.**

7 **Practise and take turns to retell Sofia's anecdote.**

- Use the pictures in Activity 1 to help you.
- Use the key sentences in Activity 3.
- Give the story background. Say *when* and *where it happened* and *what you were doing*.
- Remember to use the past continuous and the past simple. Use connectives such as *first, next, finally, and, but, so* and *when*.
- Use some of the expressions in Activity 5 to create emotion when telling your anecdote.

8 **Prepare a short anecdote about something that happened to you.**

a Choose a situation.

A holiday adventure A scary experience A school trip

b Write answers to these questions to help you plan your anecdote.
1 Where were you?
2 What were you doing?
3 What happened?
4 How did you feel?
5 What was the outcome?

c Take turns with a partner to tell your anecdote.
Remember to use the past simple, past continuous and connectives.

> 6.4 Lessons in life

We are going to...

- **plan and write a short story with a proverb.**

1   Talk: Proverbs are very old sayings that give us advice about life.
    What do you think these proverbs mean?

    A   Think before you speak   B   Practice makes perfect

2   Read **the story. What is the missing proverb at the end?**
    Choose A or B from Activity 1.

Feathers in the Wind

There **was** a girl who loved to gossip. Every day she
sat at her desk with her friends gossiping about the bad
things she thought other people did. 'Can you believe
he did that?' 'Can you believe she said that?' 'Did you see
what **she was wearing?'** … on and on she gossiped.

`past simple`   `past continuous`

One day her teacher gave her a cushion **and** told her to go
outside, 'Cut it open and throw all the feathers into the wind,' he said.

'Why?' she asked.

`connectives`

'Just do as I say,' said the teacher.

The girl went outside and cut open the cushion with a
pair of scissors. All the feathers were quickly blown by
the wind until they were out of sight.

'Now,' said the teacher. 'I'd like you to go and bring all
the feathers back.'

'I can't,' said the girl. 'They have been blown everywhere.
I'll never be able to bring them back.'

The teacher looked at the girl. 'And so it is with words
and gossip,' he told her. 'Words once spoken can never
be taken back. They can travel far and can do great harm.
From now on I want you to _____.'
And she did.

3   Read the story again and complete the information.

Story notes

a   The story has got more than two **characters**: _____, _____ and _____.

b   The **setting** is _____.

c   The **problem** is _____.

d   What happens in order to resolve the problem?

e   The **resolution** is _____.

4   Word study: **What do you think these proverbs mean? Do you agree with them?**

'Many hands make light work.'   'It takes a village to raise a child.'

'A problem shared is a problem halved.'

'Talk does not cook rice.'   'A man's home is his castle.'

5   **Write a short story. Choose one of the proverbs in Activity 4.**

Step 1:	Make notes on the characters. Describe them. Where is the story set? Describe the setting.
Step 2:	Explain the situation or problem and what happens in order to resolve it.
Step 3:	How does the story end? What is the resolution? How does the person or people feel? Remember to use direct speech, past simple and past continuous. Use connectives.
Step 4:	Swap stories with your partner – can they guess which proverb it matches?

Writing tip

Punctuation: Direct speech

Use direct speech in a story to make it sound more real. Look at how direct speech is punctuated in the story.

'Can you believe he did that?' she said. 'I can't,' said the girl.

- We use speech marks (' ') at the beginning and the end of the sentence.
- Question marks (?) commas (,) and exclamation marks (!) go inside the speech marks.

> 6.5 *The Little Prince*

We are going to...

- **read and enjoy a story about a small boy from another planet.**

 1 **Read and listen: Where do you think the little prince is from?**
Read and listen to Extract 1 from *The Little Prince*.
What surprises him about the Earth?

The Little Prince

So once he reached Earth, the little prince was quite surprised not to see anyone. He was beginning to fear he had come to the wrong planet, when a moon-colored loop uncoiled on the sand.

'Good evening,' the little prince said, just in case.

'Good evening,' said the snake.

'What planet have I landed on?' asked the little prince.

'On the planet Earth, in Africa,' the snake replied.

'Ah!... And there are no people on Earth?'

'It's the desert here. There are no people in the desert. Earth is very big,' said the snake.

The little prince sat down on a rock and looked up into the sky.

2 **Read again and circle the correct answer.**

a   The prince is on the wrong planet.
b   He thought there would be people on the Earth.

3 Read and listen to Extract 2 and answer the questions.

a How does the little prince describe the snake?

b The snake speaks in riddles. Can you find two riddles?

'I wonder,' he said,' if the stars are lit up so that each of us can find his own, someday. Look at my planet – it's just over-head. But so far away!'

'It's lovely,' the snake said. 'What have you come to Earth for?'

'I'm having difficulties with a flower,' the little prince said.

'Ah!' said the snake.

And they were both silent.

'Where are the people?' The little prince finally **resumed** the conversation. 'It's a little lonely in the desert…'

'It's also lonely with people,' said the snake.

The little prince looked at the snake for a long time. 'You're a funny creature,' he said at last, 'no thicker than a finger.'

'But I'm more powerful than a king's finger,' the snake said. The little prince smiled.

'You're not very powerful… You don't even have feet. You couldn't travel very far.'

'I can take you further than a ship,' the snake said. He coiled around the little prince's ankle, like a golden bracelet. 'Anyone I touch, I send back to the land from which he came,' the snake went on.

'But you're innocent, and you come from a star…'

The little prince made no reply.

'I feel sorry for you, being so weak on this granite earth,' said the snake.

'I can help you, someday, if you grow too **homesick** for your own planet. I can…'

'Oh, I understand just what you mean,' said the little prince, 'but why do you always speak in riddles?'

'I **solve** them all,' said the snake.

And they were both silent.

4 Read and listen to Extract 3. How does the flower describe men? How is her life different from that of men? Talk with a partner.

Chapter 18

The little prince crossed the desert and encountered only one flower. A flower with three petals – a flower of no consequence…
    'Good morning,' said the little prince.
    'Good morning,' said the flower.
    'Where are the people?' the little prince inquired **politely.**
    The flower had one day seen a caravan passing.
    'People? There are six or seven of them, I believe, in existence. I caught sight of them years ago. But you never know where to find them. The wind blows them away. They have no roots, which **hampers** them a good deal.'
    'Good-bye,' said the little prince.
    'Good-bye,' said the flower.

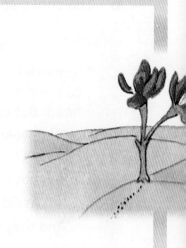

 5 Read and listen to Extract 4 and answer the questions.

a   Who did the little prince speak to on top of the mountain?
b   What adjectives does he use to describe the Earth?
c   What's his opinion of the Earth?

Chapter 19

After that, the little prince climbed a high mountain. The only mountains he had ever known were the three volcanoes, which came up to his knee. And he used the extinct volcano as a footstool. 'From a mountain as high as this one,' he said to himself, 'I'll get a view of the whole planet and all the people on it…' But he saw nothing but rocky peaks as sharp as needles.
    'Hello,' he said, just in case.
    'Hello... hello... hello…,' the **echo** answered.
    'Who are you?' said the little prince.
    'Who are you? – Who are you? – Who are you?' the echo answered.
    'Let's be friends. I'm lonely,' he said.
    'I'm lonely… I'm lonely… I'm lonely..,' the echo answered.
    'What a peculiar planet!' he thought. 'It's all dry and sharp and hard. And people here have no imagination. They repeat whatever you say to them. Where I live I had a flower: She always spoke first…'

6 Read the description of a simile. What does 'like a golden bracelet' describe in the story?

> A **simile** is a comparison between two things with a similar characteristic. We use *like* or *as* to compare them. They are used to give the reader a good picture of what is being described.

7 Word study: Can you find another simile in the story? What does it describe? Many cultures use different words to compare things that are similar. Are there any differences in your language and culture?

8 Match the two parts of the sentence to form a simile.

1	He cries like a...		a	stone.
2	It cuts like a...		b	wind.
3	She runs like the...		c	knife.
4	He eats like a...		d	glove.
5	It sinks like a...		e	baby.
6	It fits like a...		f	horse.

9 What do these riddles describe in the story?

  a   I am more powerful than the finger of a king. A snake
  b   I'm tall, but I'm not a skyscraper. You can climb me, but I'm not a tree.
  c   Nobody saw me, but everybody heard me.
  d   I shine like a jewel in the night.
  e   I'm a blue sheet which covers the world.

10 Write a simple riddle about nature. Choose from these options.
   In groups, read and guess what each riddle is describing.

 a river   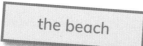 the beach    a forest    a volcano

11 Values: Belonging and friendship

  a   Why did the Prince travel to the Earth?
  b   Why do you think the flower was important to him?
  c   How did he feel on Earth? Did he like being there?
  d   What do you think the story tells us about the importance of where we are from and friendship?

> 6.6 Project challenge

Project A: Create an Aboriginal dot painting for a class mural

1. What can you see in this painting? Use the symbols on page 97 to describe the scene or the story.

2. Plan your painting. Decide on the following:
   - Think about the scene or story it is going to tell.
   - Decide on the symbols you want to use.
   - Think about a title for your painting.
   - Organise the things you will need – card/paper, coloured pencils or paints.

3. First, sketch out your scene in pencil.

4. Next, paint your scene using dots and symbols from page 97.

5. Write the title and a short description of your scene to stick alongside your painting.

6. Display your painting on the large Aboriginal Art class mural.

Project B: Perform a play *The Little Prince*

1   In groups of four or five choose one of these parts.
    (Remember some parts have much more to read than others!)

    | Narrator | The little prince | The snake | The flower | The mountain (echo) |

2   Highlight in colour the parts of the story you will read,
    or write them on a piece of paper.

    Narrator: blue   Prince: yellow   Snake: green

    When the little prince arrived on the Earth, he was
    very much surprised not to see any people. He
    was beginning to be afraid he had come to the
    wrong planet, when a coil of gold, the colour of the
    moonlight, flashed across the sand.

    'Good evening,'   said the little prince courteously.

    'Good evening,'   said the snake.

3   Practise reading your part.
    Remember to use your voice to show surprise, disbelief or sadness.

4   Organise the setting in class or on the stage at school.
    Bring in props. Make a snake and a flower mask.

5   If you have a small part, you can be the stage director. Tell the characters
    where to stand and how to gesture with their hands as they speak.

6   Perform your play to the rest of the class.

Did you have any problems while doing your project?
How did you solve them?

❯ 6.7 What do you know now?

What can we learn about life from stories?

1 Look back at the unit and answer the question above

2 Complete these sentences with a connective: so, and, then, but

a   I wanted to play outside _____ it was raining.

b   There was something moving in the box _____ I opened it.

c   First, I went to the library for a book _____ I went home to start reading it.

d   There were lots of dogs _____ cats in the enormous garden.

3 Use your imagination. Complete this sentence about *The Book Thief's* intentions on page 95.
The figure was looking for...

4 Write three sentences in the past continuous to explain what your family were doing when the phone rang last night

When the phone rang, I was doing my homework.

5 What lesson did the girl learn in the story *Feathers in the Wind?*

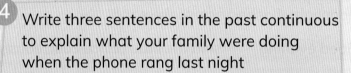

Look what I can do		
Write or show examples in your notebook.	😐	🙂
I can talk about different types of stories.	○	○
I can understand the meaning of Aboriginal symbols in art.	○	○
I can use the past simple and past continuous to talk about events and actions in the past.	○	○
I can tell an anecdote about an experience I've had.	○	○
I can write a short story using direct speech.	○	○
I can understand a story *The Little Prince.*	○	○

Check your progress 2

1 **Find three words for each category in the word puzzle.**

Stories   Celebrations   The Brain

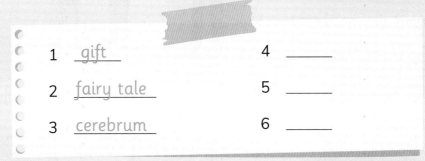

2 **Match the definitions to the words.**

a   a type of present

b   an involuntary action

c   something which you burn to make light

d   a magazine or book telling a story in pictures with some writing

e   something which controls the flow of messages between the brain and the rest of the body

f   a short story about a moral

3 **Now add two more words to each category in Activity 1.**

4 **Play a defining game. Follow the instructions.**

a   In pairs, choose and write six words from Units 5, 6 and 7. Number them 1–6.

> 1 _gift_   4 _____
>
> 2 _fairy tale_   5 _____
>
> 3 _cerebrum_   6 _____

b   Join with another pair. Take turns to throw the dice and use that number on the key below to find a way to define the word. The winner is the first to get 6 points.

Key:

1 = draw   2 = define   3 = mime

4 = spell   5 = free choice (any word)   6 = win a free point!

5   Write a short story using the sentence prompts.
    Use the past simple and the past continuous.
    You can use these words to help you.

> **Place:** at school, in town, at the park, in the sports centre, on holiday, at home
>
> **Actions:** playing sport, eating dinner, studying, riding my bike, sleeping
>
> **Adjectives:** amazing, scary, incredible, magical
>
> This story is about when I _____ (past simple). I _____ (past continuous) when _____ (past simple). What happened next was _____. Suddenly, I _____. It was a/an _____ (adjective) experience.

6   Read and compare stories with a partner.

7   Use the pictures to help you finish these zero conditional sentences.

    a   When it's cold, I...

    b   My heart beats faster, if I...

    c   If my friend yawns, I...

8   Now write five zero conditional sentences of your own with these adjectives

excited   tired   hot   happy   angry   thirsty

When I'm excited, I jump up and down!

9   Find someone else in the class who has similar sentences to you.

7 ▶ Ancient Rome and Egypt

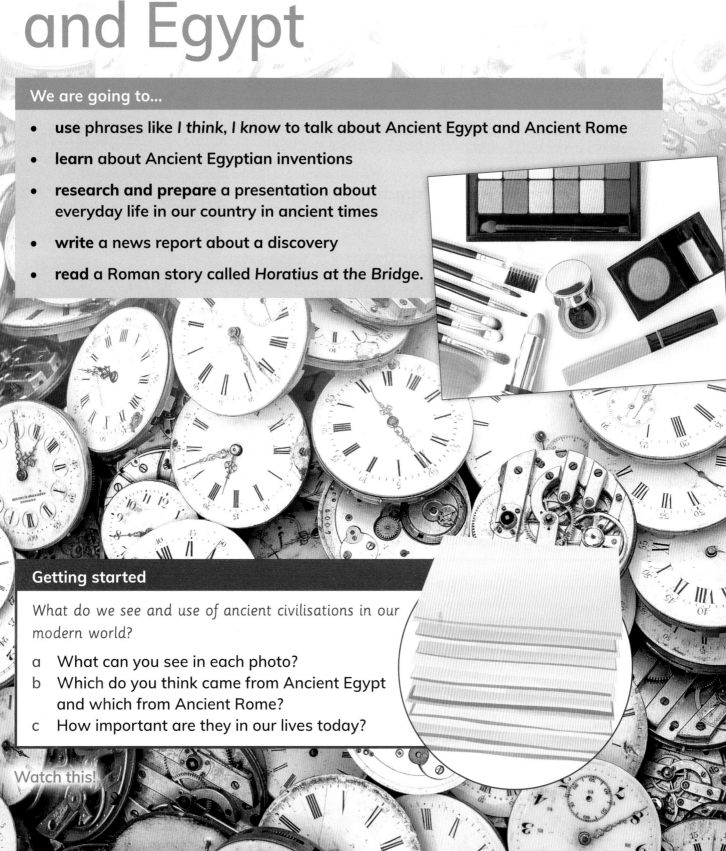

We are going to...

- **use** phrases like *I think, I know* to talk about Ancient Egypt and Ancient Rome
- **learn** about Ancient Egyptian inventions
- **research and prepare** a presentation about everyday life in our country in ancient times
- **write** a news report about a discovery
- **read** a Roman story called *Horatius at the Bridge*.

Getting started

What do we see and use of ancient civilisations in our modern world?

a   What can you see in each photo?
b   Which do you think came from Ancient Egypt and which from Ancient Rome?
c   How important are they in our lives today?

Watch this!

> 7.1 Why were these civilisations important?

We are going to...

- use phrases like *I think, I know* to talk about Ancient Egypt and Ancient Rome.

a

1 Talk: Do you recognise these structures and buildings? Where can you find them? Do you know which civilisations built them?

b

c

41 **2** Listen to the information. Match the names with the pictures.

| The Colosseum | The Pyramids | The Sphinx | **An aqueduct** |

41 **3** Match the sentences with a structure or building from Activity 1. Listen again and check your answers.

1 These were the stone tombs of the Pharaohs.
2 People believed that this creature guarded the tomb of the Pharaoh.
3 It's quite similar in shape to a modern football stadium.
4 They were built to provide a fresh water supply.
5 It was a place where people went for entertainment.

d

> **Use of English – Expressing opinions and beliefs using *think, know, believe***
>
> **People believed that** this creature guarded the Pharaoh's tomb.

4   Use of English: **Look at the Use of English box and match the sentence halves.**

1 I think that…	a the Sphinx guarded the tomb of the King.
2 I know that…	b the Colosseum is similar in shape to a football stadium.
3 I believe that…	c aqueducts transported fresh water to Roman cities.

5   Talk: **Do you think these facts are true or false?**
**Use *I think that*, *I believe that* or *I know that* to talk about them
with a partner. Use these pictures to help you make an opinion.**

Is it true that …

a   all the organs were taken out of the Pharaoh's body before mummification?
b   the Ancient Egyptians used pictures and not words to show ideas?
c   zero is not used in Roman numerals?
d   it took one month to make a mummy?

6   Vocabulary: **Match the definitions with the correct picture.**
Check your opinions from Activity 5.

a   This is where Romans liked to wash and bathe.

b   A slave who fought against wild animals in an amphitheatre.

c   These are the numbers used by Romans. There are seven digits and no zero.

d   The liver, stomach and lungs of a mummy, but not the heart were put in this.

e   This is Egyptian writing. They used pictures to show objects, ideas and sounds.

f   This is the body of a person that has been preserved. It took three months to do.

a canopic jar

a mummy

a gladiator

Roman baths

hieroglyphics

IX
IV
XC

Roman numerals

> 7.2 Egyptian inventions

We are going to...

- **learn about Ancient Egyptian inventions.**

 1 **Read and listen: What did the Egyptians invent?**
Listen and read the text then match each part to the pictures.
Do any of the inventions surprise you?

a    b 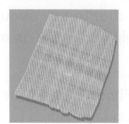   c    d

2 **Read the text again. Answer these questions.**

a   What kind of infections did the Egyptians have medicine for?
b   What did they make toothpaste out of?
c   What are hieroglyphics?
d   What did the Egyptians write on? What was it made from?
e   What in your opinion is the strangest invention described in the text?

> **Reading tip**
>
> Work out words from context.
>
> Use key words to help you. Can you work out the meaning of **reed** and **scribe**?

 3 **Listen and match the instructions to two of the inventions in Activity 1.**

4 **Talk: Play a game. Which invention is it? Use these verbs to give an instruction about making papyrus paper, toothpaste or medicine. Take turns with a partner to guess the experiment.**

> **Use of English – Imperative forms**
>
> Imperatives are used to give instructions or commands.
> **Crush** some rock salt.   **Mix** with honey

| cut | pick | mix | **crush** | place | flatten | write |

Cut into strips.

I know! Papyrus paper!

Egyptian inventions

Medicine

What do you think the first medicines were made from?

Well, the Ancient Egyptians developed medicines for all kinds of infections. For the eyes they mixed honey with brains and a cooked mouse was used to help cure coughs!

Paper

How do you think the first paper was made?

The Egyptians were the creators of the first form of paper made from a tall reed called Papyrus, which grows along the banks of the River Nile. They used the inner part of the plant, which they cut into strips, flattened and dried for the scribes to write on.

Hieroglyphics

Did you know that the Ancient Egyptians were the inventors of the first form of writing?

They wrote using picture words called hieroglyphics. Thousands of symbols were used to represent sounds, letters and, often, whole words. Scribes studied for years to learn all the symbols.

Toothpaste

Do you ever think about where toothpaste comes from?

The Ancient Egyptians liked to look after their teeth, so they invented a peculiar paste made with salt, mint, pepper and dried flowers.

(verb)	(noun)	(person)
invent	invention	inventor
create	creation	creator
develop	development	developer

> 7.3 Everyday life in Ancient Rome

We are going to...

- research and prepare a presentation about everyday life in our country in ancient times.

1 **Talk:** What's everyday life like in your town or city?
In pairs, talk about the subjects below.

| clothes | food | transport | **houses** | jobs | **pets** | entertainment |

2 **Vocabulary:** What was everyday life like in Ancient Rome? How is it different to life in your town today? Can you find the words below in the picture?

| togas | tunics | bread | **sandals** | baths | **chariot** |
| gladiator | **farmer** | **soldier** | **merchant** | engineer | villas |

3 Listen to Part 1 of Ryan's presentation about life in Ancient Rome. Order the parts of his presentation below. Listen carefully for clues (*food*, *jobs*).

a Typical food

b Common jobs/ professions

c Roman houses

d Entertainment

e Clothes

 4 How does Ancient Rome still influence modern-day culture?
Listen to Part 2 of Ryan's presentation. Complete the sentences.

1 The Romans showed us how to build...

2 They showed us how to transport water via...

3 They showed us how to heat...

4 We still play Roman games such as...

5 Roman numerals are used on...

 5 Pronunciation: Listen to how we pronounce *soldier* and *gladiator*.
Does the **-er** and **-or** sound the same or different?

 6 Listen to Part 2 of Ryan's presentation. Write down two more professions that end in **-er**. Can you think of four more jobs that end in **-er**?

7 Word study: Can you work out Roman numerals? Use the key below.
Write Roman numerals for your partner to work out.

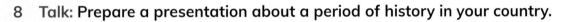

1 I	3 III	4 IV	5 V	6 VI	7 VII	8 VIII	9 IX
10 X	15 XV	50 L	90 XC	100 C	500 D	1000 M	

8 Talk: Prepare a presentation about a period of history in your country.

- Research and take notes about: *clothes, food, housing, transport, jobs* and *entertainment*.
- Find photos or draw pictures to show the class.
- Use subordinate clauses – *I know, I believe* and *I think that* – in your presentation.
- Talk for 3 minutes about your topic.

⟩ 7.4 An amazing discovery!

We are going to...

- write a news report about a discovery.

1 **Talk: Have you ever found something interesting or of value, perhaps on a beach or in an old toy box? Talk about it in groups.**

2 **Read the news report. What was discovered? Why was it such an amazing discovery?**

KING TUT'S TOMB DISCOVERED!

Yesterday, on the 24th November 1922, the archaeologist Howard Carter discovered the tomb of King Tutankhamun in the Valley of the Kings where many of the pharaohs were buried. The tomb was so small that it was not discovered for over 3 000 years!

`past simple`

Tutankhamun became Pharaoh of Egypt when his father died in 1337 BCE. He was only nine years old! His death at the age of eighteen is still a mystery to scientists. Some believe he died from an infection in a broken leg. Others think he died from a blow to the head.

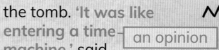

Howard Carter and his team were amazed by the treasures inside the tomb. 'It was like entering a time-machine,' said Carter. 'We can now learn so much about daily life in Ancient Egypt.'

`an opinion`

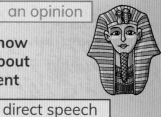

`direct speech`

More than 3 000 treasures were found in the tomb.

`a fact`

On the walls there were hieroglyphics, a golden chariot, weapons, jewellery and a throne. There was even a board game to play Senet – a popular game in Ancient Egypt. The most incredible discovery though, was the mummy of Tutankhamun and the solid gold face mask.

3 Read: **Which of these sentences are fact (F) and which are opinion (O)?**

    a   More than 3 000 treasures were found in the tomb. ___F___

    b   Some believe he died from an infection. _____

    c   Tutankhamun became king when his father died. _____

    d   'It was like entering a time machine.' _____

    e   Others think he died from a blow to the head. _____

4 Write: **Match the sentences to a category.**

| A fact | An opinion | A headline | A quotation |

    a   Young boy finds gold Roman coins in his garden.

    b   'It was the most beautiful thing I had ever seen!' said Ana.

    c   Some people can't believe he found the treasure.

    d   Yesterday morning, the treasure chest was found on the beach.

> **Language focus**
>
> **Prepositions of time, location and position**
>
> Yesterday, **on** 24th November 1922... (time) ...**in** the Valley of the Kings. (location)

5 Use of English: **Find more examples of prepositions of time, location and position in the text.**

6 Write **a news report about a real or invented discovery.**

Step 1: Research and planning	Use a mind map to help you organise your facts and ideas.
Step 2: Writing	• Think of an interesting headline for your report. • Use past tenses to describe the events. • Include quotations from the person who made the discovery. • Include facts and opinions.
Step 3: Display	• Draw pictures of the discovery or find photos online. • Display your work in the classroom.

7 **Now you have finished your report, check that you have included everything on the checklist.**

Checklist ✓	
Use past tenses.	☐
Use past tenses.	☐
Use some direct speech..	☐
Include facts and opinions.	☐

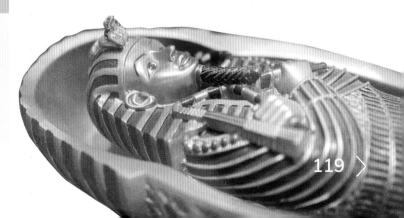

> 7.5 Horatius at the Bridge

We are going to...

- **read a Roman story called *Horatius at the Bridge*.**

1 Talk: Imagine you are a child living in the ancient city of Rome.
Where do you live? What is your everyday life like? Do you think life was
more dangerous then? How do you think the Romans protected their cities?

 2 **Read and listen** to the first part of the story and check your ideas.

Horatius at the Bridge

Once there was a war between the Roman people and the Etruscans who lived in the towns on the other side of the Tiber River. Porsena, the King of the Etruscans, had a great army, and marched towards Rome with its huge walls and guards. The city had never been in such great danger.

The Romans did not have very many fighting men at that time, and they knew that they were not strong enough to defeat the Etruscans in a battle. So they stayed inside the city walls, and set guards to watch the roads.

One morning the guards saw the Porsena army coming over the hills from the north. There were thousands of horsemen and footmen, and they were marching straight towards Rome.

'What shall we do?' said the white-haired Fathers who made the laws for the Roman people. 'If they get to the bridge, we cannot stop them from crossing; and then what hope will there be for the town?'

Now, among the guards at the bridge, there was a brave man named Horatius. When he saw that the Etruscans were near, he called out to the Romans who were behind him.

'Cut down the bridge as quickly as you can!' he shouted. 'I, with the two men who stand by me, will protect you.'

3 **Answer the questions.**

a   Why was Rome in danger?
b   Who were the white-haired fathers?
c   What were they worried about?
d   What did Horatius command the other guards to do?

4 **What do you think will happen next? Read and listen. Check your ideas.**

Then, with their shields and their long spears in their hands, the three brave men stood in the road, and kept back the horsemen who Porsena had sent to take the bridge.

On the bridge the Romans cut at the beams and posts. Their axes rang, the chips flew fast; and soon it trembled, and was ready to fall.

'Come back! Come back, and save your lives!' they shouted to Horatius and the two other guards.

But just then Porsena's horsemen dashed toward them again.

'Run for your lives!' said Horatius to his friends. 'I will keep the road.'

They turned, and ran back across the bridge. They had just reached the other side when there was a crashing of wooden beams. The bridge fell over to one side, and then fell with a great splash into the water.

When Horatius heard the sound, he knew that the city was safe. He moved slowly backwards until he stood on the river's bank. One of Porsena's soldiers threw a spear which hit him in the eye, but he did not stop. He threw his spear at the horseman, and then he turned quickly around. He saw the white porch of his own home among the trees on the other side of the stream.

He **leaped** into the deep, **swift** stream. He still had his heavy armour on; and when he sank out of sight, no one thought that he would ever be seen again. But he was a strong man, and the best swimmer in Rome. The next minute he rose. He was half-way across the river, and safe from the **spears** which Porsena's soldiers were throwing at him.

Soon he reached the other side, where his friends stood ready to help him. Shout after shout greeted him as he climbed upon the bank. Then Porsena's men shouted too because they had never seen a man so selfless and strong as Horatius. They were defeated, but Horatius had been so brave that they could not help but praise him.

5 **Read and answer true (T) or false (F).**

a The Romans didn't want a battle. _____

b The two other guards made it back across the bridge. _____

c The city wasn't safe when the bridge fell into the river. _____

d Horatius fell into the river and wasn't seen again. _____

e Horatius helped prevent the Etruscans from entering the city. _____

The Romans were very grateful to Horatius for saving their city. They called him Horatius Cocles, which meant the 'one-eyed Horatius', because he had lost an eye defending the bridge; they made a statue of brass to honour him and they gave him as much land as he could plough in a day.

6 **Talk: Why did the people of Rome call Horatius 'Horatius Cocles'?**

7 **Word study: Match the words in blue in the text to the definitions below.**

'Alone stood brave Horatius.'—P. 38.

   a   to jump
   b   to run quickly
   c   a tool for cutting things down
   d   fast
   e   thankful
   f   a weapon

8 **Put these sentences in order and summarise the story.**

   a   He leaped into the river and swam to safety. _____
   b   The Etruscan army marched to the city of Rome. __1__
   c   The guards cut down the wooden bridge to the city. _____
   d   A statue was made in Horatius' honour. __8__
   e   Horatius was hit by an Etruscan spear. _____
   f   Before the bridge fell, two of the guards crossed it back to the city. _____
   g   Horatius and two other guards stood in the road on the other side of the bridge. _____
   h   Both the Romans and the Etruscan army cheered Horatius for his bravery and strength. _____

9 **Values: Being Selfless (thinking of others' needs before your own)**

   a   How does Horatius think of others before himself?
   b   Why do you think Horatius was cheered by both the Romans and the Etruscan army?
   c   What can we learn from this?
   d   When are you selfless?

⟩ 7.6 Project challenge

Project A: Write about an ancient building or statue

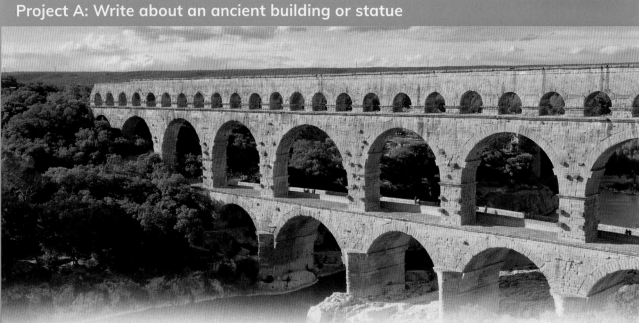

1 Find out about an ancient building or statue in your country.

2 Do research online and find out the following information:

- What year/century was it built?

- Who built it?

- What was it built for?

- Write about its history.

- Is it still used or admired by people today?

3 If possible, visit the building or statue. Draw a picture of it or take a photo.

4 Write down adjectives to describe it.

5 What is it made of?

6 What is your opinion of it?

7 Present your work to your class or post it on the school/class blog.

Project B: Egyptian hieroglyphics – break the code!

1 Look at these symbols used in Ancient Egyptian writing.

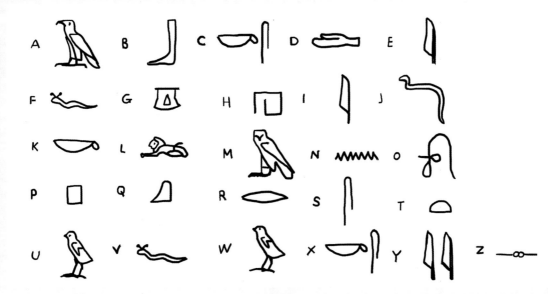

2 Can you read these coded words?

3 Write your own codes for your classmates to guess. You could write your name, your favourite food, sport or singer in hieroglyphics.

Did you find out anything surprising when doing your project?

❯ 7.7 What do you know now?

What can we see of ancient civilisations in our culture today?

1 Look back at the unit and answer the question above.

2 Write a definition for the following words:

> pyramid   Roman numerals
>
> **hieroglyphics   pharaoh**

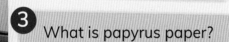

3 What is papyrus paper?

4 What were the ingredients of Ancient Egyptian toothpaste?

5 Answer these questions:
a What did people wear in Ancient Rome?
b What did they eat?
c What were common jobs and professions?

6 Write these numbers in Roman numerals
a 17   b 23
c 14   d 115
e 1550

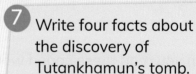

7 Write four facts about the discovery of Tutankhamun's tomb.

Look what I can do

Write or show examples in your notebook.

I can use subordinate clauses to talk about Ancient Egypt and Ancient Rome.   ◯ ◯

I can read and understand a text about Egyptian inventions.   ◯ ◯

I can give a presentation about life in my country in ancient times.   ◯ ◯

I can write a news report.   ◯ ◯

I can understand a story about Horatius at the Bridge.   ◯ ◯

8 Rainforests

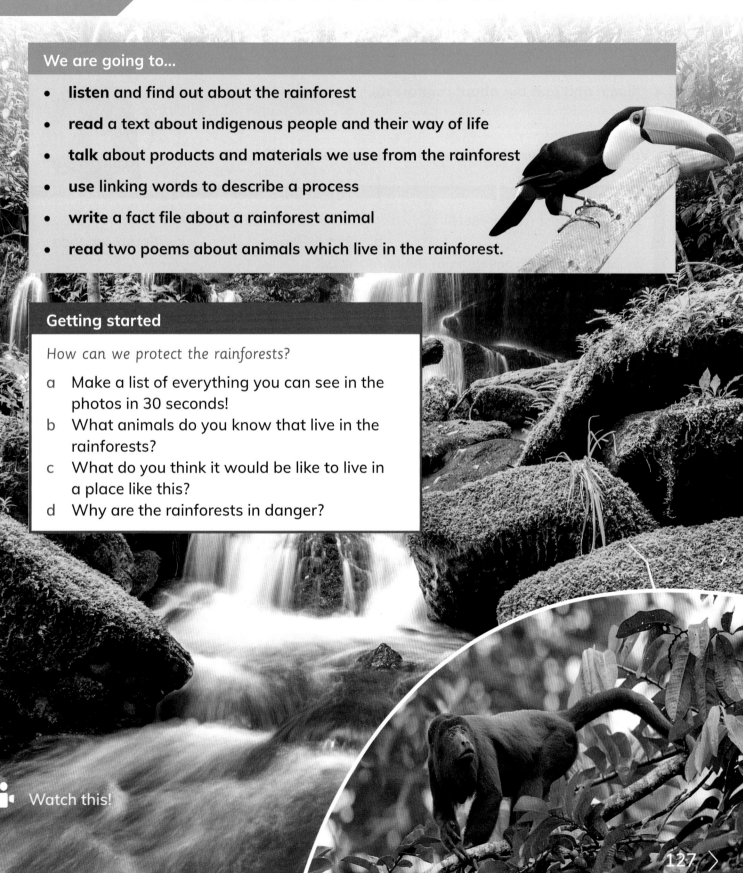

We are going to...

- **listen** and find out about the rainforest
- **read** a text about indigenous people and their way of life
- **talk** about products and materials we use from the rainforest
- **use** linking words to describe a process
- **write** a fact file about a rainforest animal
- **read** two poems about animals which live in the rainforest.

Getting started

How can we protect the rainforests?

a   Make a list of everything you can see in the photos in 30 seconds!

b   What animals do you know that live in the rainforests?

c   What do you think it would be like to live in a place like this?

d   Why are the rainforests in danger?

Watch this!

⟩ 8.1 What do you know about rainforests?

We are going to...

- **listen and find out about rainforests.**

1 Vocabulary: What do you know about rainforests? Try this quiz.

1 The largest rainforest is in...
   a Africa   b Asia   c South America
2 How tall can trees grow in the rainforests?
   a more than 30 metres   b less than 20 metres   c 15 metres
3 What's the top part of the rainforest called?
   a the forest floor   b the canopy   c the understory
4 Rainforests are home to what percentage of the world's plants, animals and insects?
   a 20%   b 50%   c 80%
5 Every second, humans cut down an area of the rainforest the size of...
   a an Olympic swimming pool   b a football pitch   c a basketball court

2 Listen and check your answers to the quiz.

3 Listen again and label the picture of the rainforest using these words.

   a forest floor   b understory   c canopy

Listening tip

Predicting content

Thinking about the topic and the things you know about it before you listen can help you understand the topic better.

1

2

3

4 Listen again and answer these questions.

    a   What is a rainforest?
    b   What lives in the rainforest?
    c   Why are rainforests important to us?
    d   What is happening to the rainforests?

5 Word study: Read this part of the transcript again about the importance of the rainforest. Match the words in blue with the definitions below.

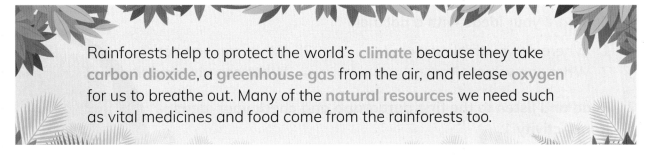

Rainforests help to protect the world's climate because they take carbon dioxide, a greenhouse gas from the air, and release oxygen for us to breathe out. Many of the natural resources we need such as vital medicines and food come from the rainforests too.

    a   a gas that we breathe out
    b   weather conditions in a particular area
    c   a gas that keeps heat in the Earth's atmosphere
    d   things such as water, forests and minerals which can be used by people
    e   a gas that we breathe in

6 Talk: What's it like living in a rainforest? Imagine life there and make a list about the good and the bad things. What would you miss the most? Compare with a partner.

I think it would be good because you breathe fresh air.

I think it would be bad because there's no Wi-Fi!

129 >

〉 8.2 Indigenous people and their way of life

We are going to...

- **read a text about indigenous people and their way of life.**

1 **Talk: Close your eyes and listen to the rainforest sounds.
Compare your ideas with a partner.**

1 Where do you think you are?
2 What can you see?
3 What can you hear?
4 What can you smell?

2 **Read and listen to the first paragraph and check your ideas
from Activity 1.**

The rainforest is a very wet, humid place. It's often quite dark because
of the dense canopy of trees above. The smell is strong here: wet wood,
soil and sweet smelling flowers. The noise is incredible! You can hear the
humming of the cicadas and the **buzzing** of the insects. Birds are
chirping and monkeys are **howling** from high above.

This is the home of the Yanomami tribe who have lived in the Amazon rainforest
in South America for hundreds of years. Yanomami means 'human being' in their language and
they survive by living off the local land. They gather fruits from the forests and like to eat seeds,
nuts and honey.

They live in small villages of between 40 and 300 people. They build shelters called 'shabonos'
around a circular structure which are made from tree trunks, palm leaves and grass. They hunt
monkeys, deer, tapir and armadillos and eat vegetables which they have grown too.

The Yanomami way of life has been in danger since men began cutting down
huge areas of the rainforest for farm land and mining. This means they
have less land to hunt on and mining pollutes the rivers they drink. As a
result many of the Yanomami indigenous people are losing their homes
and their way of life.

Key words: Nature sounds

humming: the sound some insects make with their wings
buzzing: the sound a bee, a wasp or a mosquito makes
chirping: the sound a bird makes
howling: the sound a monkey makes

 3 Now read and listen to all of the text. Complete the chart with information about the Yanomami's way of life.

Habitat	Wet...
Housing	
Diet	
Dangers	

Use of English – Present perfect

For is used to talk about a period of time.

Since is used to talk about the point from which something started.

The Yanomami tribe **has lived** in the rainforest **for** hundreds of years.
The Yanomami way of life **has been** in danger **since** men began cutting down huge areas of the rainforest.

---

4 Use of English: Can you find another example of the present perfect in the text?

5 Talk: What's the difference between your lifestyle and the Yanomami's? What challenges do you think they face?

› 8.3 Rainforest resources

We are going to...

- talk about products and materials we use from the rainforest.

1 **Word study: Which of these products do you have in your home right now? Match the words to the pictures. What do you think they have in common?**

1 cinnamon 2 a bouncy ball 3 bananas 4 coffee

a    b    c    d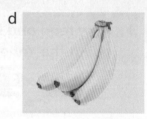

 2 **Listen and check your ideas. Does anything surprise you?**

 3 **What other products come from the rainforests? Listen again and write a list.**

 4 **Listen to a class presentation and label the pictures a–d about the process of making natural rubber.**

5   Write **four simple sentences using these verbs to describe each part of the process.**

roll   catch   cut   remove

> ### Use of English – Adverbs of degree: *quite, a little, very, extremely*
>
> These adverbs give us more information about adjectives and their strength.
>
> ...a white liquid which is **very milky** called latex.
> The rubber tree produces **extremely large** amounts.

 6   Use of English: **Listen again and find an example with** *quite* and *a little*.

> ### Speaking tip
>
> We use linking words to help sequence information.
>
> *First of all, then, next, finally*

 7   Pronunciation: **Listen to these sentences.**
Which word or words are stressed?
Practise with a partner.

First of all, part of the bark is cut off...

Then, a container is placed under the cut...

8   Present it! **Write about how another rainforest product is processed**
(such as coffee or cinnamon).

- Investigate online (find interesting photos and learn about the process).
- Make notes about the process.
- Think of verbs you need to describe each part.
- Use linking words such as *First of all, then, next* and *finally* to order the information.
- Use adverbs of degree.
- Practise your description. Remember to stress the important information.
- Use photos and pictures to illustrate the process.
- Present your investigative work to the class.

❯ 8.4 Rainforest animals

We are going to...

- write a fact file about a rainforest animal.

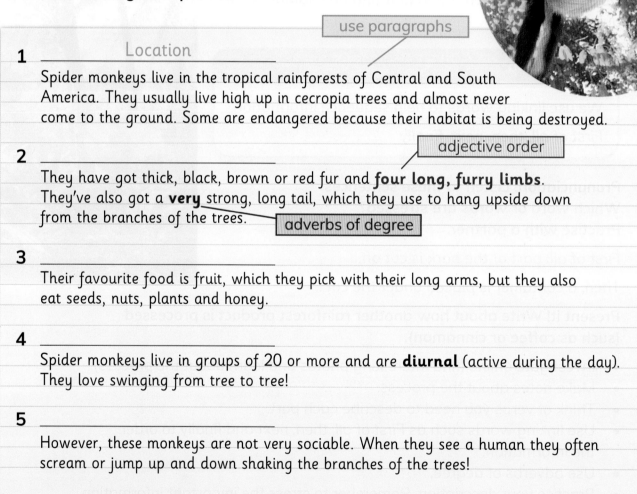

1 What kind of animals live in rainforests?
Can you remember which layer of the rainforest they live in?
Write a list and compare with a partner.

2 Read: Mina's description of the spider monkey.
Is it an endangered species?

> use paragraphs

1 _____ Location _____

Spider monkeys live in the tropical rainforests of Central and South
America. They usually live high up in cecropia trees and almost never
come to the ground. Some are endangered because their habitat is being destroyed.

> adjective order

2 _____

They have got thick, black, brown or red fur and **four long, furry limbs**.
They've also got a **very** strong, long tail, which they use to hang upside down
from the branches of the trees.

> adverbs of degree

3 _____

Their favourite food is fruit, which they pick with their long arms, but they also
eat seeds, nuts, plants and honey.

4 _____

Spider monkeys live in groups of 20 or more and are **diurnal** (active during the day).
They love swinging from tree to tree!

5 _____

However, these monkeys are not very sociable. When they see a human they often
scream or jump up and down shaking the branches of the trees!

3 **Choose a heading for each of the Sections 1 to 5 in the text.**

a Diet   b Appearance   c Location   d Behaviour   e Curious fact

Language focus

Adjective order

When we use more than one adjective to describe a noun, the adjectives need to be in the following order:

1		2		3		4		5		6		7		8		9
Number	→	Opinion	→	Size	→	Shape	→	Age	→	Colour	→	Origin	→	Material	→	Noun
Three		fabulous		big		fat		old		brown		Costa Rican		furry		sloths

4 **Vocabulary: Find and circle the description of the spider monkey in the text. Match the adjectives to a colour category above.**

5 **Write a fact file about a rainforest animal.**

Step 1: Research online	Make notes about the animal's: 1 Location (habitat) 2 Appearance 3 Diet 4 Behaviour 5 Curious fact
Step 2: Writing	• Remember to use correct adjective order. • Add adverbs of degree: **very** tiny ears. • Draw a picture of your animal or find a photo to stick on your fact file.
Step 3: Read and respond	Swap with a partner. Give an opinion about their animal.

6 **Now you have finished your description, check that you have included everything on the checklist.**

Checklist

Use paragraphs. ☐

Use correct adjective order. ☐

Use adverbs of degree. ☐

> 8.5 Poems: A Visit with Mr Tree Frog and *If I Were a Sloth*

We are going to...

- **read** two poems about animals which live in the rainforest.

1   Talk: What's your favourite animal? What group of animals do frogs belong to below? Think of more examples for each group.

 Reptiles    Mammals    Amphibians   Fish

 2   **Read and listen** to the poem. Match the illustrations to a line in the poem.

a

b

A visit with Mr Tree Frog

I have a tiny **buddy**,
2   Tree Frog is his name.
He flew in from Brazil
4   In his tiny toy plane

He rattles when he speaks.
6   He's greener than green grass.
He is a tree hugger
8   That really is first class.

He has **bright** orange toes
10   That **wiggle** in the night.
He's a **mellow** fellow
12   That does not like to fight.

He dines on crickets and flies,
14   And moths are for a treat.
He's not the average **guy**
16   You find on city streets.

c

d

Glossary

buddy: friend
mellow: smooth and soft
guy: man

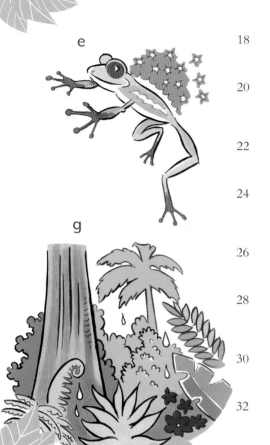

e

f

h

g

He was born in a forest,
18 A forest with **warm** rain.
He is an earthly treasure
20 That has a claim to fame.

He has a magic **slime**
22 That can **cure** laziness.
His slime can cure the world,
24 And yet he's poisonous.

His eyes are really red.
26 They pop up like **snaps**.
He **blinks** when he's resting.
28 During the day he naps.

He is here to brainstorm
30 About our planet so green.
He's a **wonder** of our world.
32 The cutest I've ever seen.

Kathy Paysen

Glossary

slime: a sticky liquid
snap: to take a lot of photos quickly

3 **Word study: Match the words in blue in the poem to the definitions below.**

a intense
b to open and close your eyes quickly
c a nice temperature

d to heal something
e to move quickly from side to side
f a surprising thing

4 **Values: Protecting animal habitats. What can you do to protect the tree frog's habitat? Tick the things you'd like to change.**

a ☐
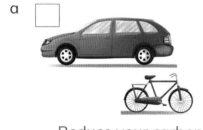
Reduce your carbon footprint

b ☐

Recycle

c ☐

Buy fair trade products

5 **Talk: What is the poet's opinion of the tree frog?
What do you think of the tree frog?**

6 Word study: Look at the pictures of the sloth.
Use adjectives to describe it. What do you think it likes doing?

57 **7** Read and listen to the poem. Put the illustrations in order.

If I were a sloth

b

1 If I were a sloth
Hanging from a tree,
I could show the world
My personality.

5 I would see the world
Hanging upside down,
Dangling like a coconut,
High above the ground.

9 I would nap all day
In the canopy,
Of the Rainforest
Crecopia trees.

13 I would move real slow,
Slow as slow can be,
Hiding from jaguar,
My fierce enemy.

17 I am nocturnal.
I only play at night.
When the sun goes down,
I like to grab a bite.

21 I can whistle like a bird.
I am really rare.
With my long, long arms,
People like to stare.

25 In my grey-green coat,
I will always thrive.
I'm a little sloth.
I make the jungle jive.

Kathy Paysen

a

c

d

e

8 Word study: **Use the correct form of the action verbs from the poem to complete the sentences. Use your dictionary to check for meaning.**

| hang | move | play | **whistle** | stare |

a Snails _____ very slowly.

b Why is that girl _____ at me? Do I look funny?

c Monkeys use their arms to _____ from tree branches.

d Children like to _____ hide and seek.

e My parrot _____ at me when I come into the room!

9 Read **the poems again and compare the tree frog and the sloth. Write T (true) or F (false).**

a They both live in the rainforest. _____
b They are both poisonous. _____
c They are both nocturnal. _____
d They both make strange noises. _____

10 Word study: **We can compare two things by using the word like. Look at the examples from the poems. Complete the similes below using your own words.**

They pop up **like** snaps.
Dangling **like** a coconut.

a The sloth is furry like…
b The sloth is lazy like…
c The frog is green like…
d The frog's slime is magic like…

11 Write **more similes about the sloth and the tree frog.**

12 Talk: **Which rainforest animal do you like best? Give reasons for your answers.**

> ## 8.6 Project challenge

Project A: Make a 3D model showing the layers of the rainforest

1 Get into groups and find the material you need to make your rainforest scene.

- Two shoe boxes
- Green crepe paper for creating the trees and the vines
- Scissors, glue, coloured pens and/or paints
- White card

2 Divide up the following tasks in your group:

a Colour/paint the shoeboxes brown or green.
(Optional: Cut out the shape of a tree trunk and branches.)
b Make trees, plants and vines using the green crepe paper and stick on the boxes.
c Draw, colour and cut out your favourite rainforest animals.
d Add your animals to the display.

3 Display and present your 3D model of the rainforest to your class. Describe the animals and plants that are in it.

Project B: Raise money to help protect the rainforests

1 As you've learned in this unit, the rainforests are in great danger.
These children have raised money to help protect the rainforest.
Match the headings to the photos.

Poetry recitals   A sponsored running race   The Great Bake Sale

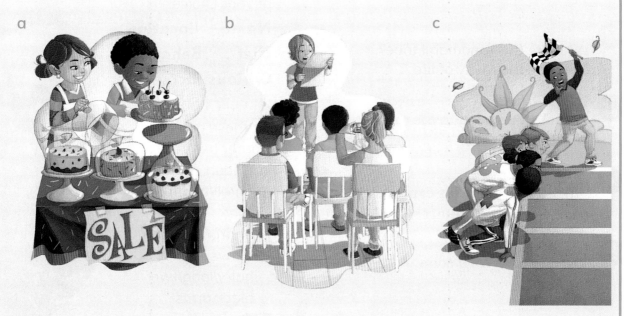

a   b   c

2 In groups, talk about which is your favourite activity above.
Discuss others ways you could raise money.

3 Vote on which fundraising activity you like best.

4 Organise your activity with the help of your teacher.
You can then donate the money you raise to conservations groups
which are working to protect the rainforest.

How well did your group work as a team? Did you have to solve
any problems? Did you find a solution?

> 8.7 What do you know now?

How can we protect the rainforests?

1 Write four important facts that you've learned about the rainforest.

2 Who are the Yanomami tribe? Describe their way of life.

3 What's happening to the rainforest? Give reasons why.

4 Write three examples explaining how people can help protect the rainforest.

5 What types of food come from the rainforest?

6 Complete these facts about a rainforest animal of your choice.
Name   Location
Diet   Behaviour
Curious fact

7 Put these adjectives in order before the final noun.
a   small/two/furry toes
b   sharp/four/long claws
c   hairy/long/two/ black arms

Look what I can do

Write or show examples in your notebook.

I can understand a scientific text about the rainforest.

I can understand a text about indigenous people and their way of life.

I can talk about the products and material we use from the rainforest.

I can describe a process using linking words.

I can write a fact file about a rainforest animal.

I can understand two poems about animals which live in the rainforest.

Animal kingdom

We are going to...

- **talk** and find out about animal habitats
- **use** modal verbs to talk about how we can protect a sea animal's habitat
- **read** a text about animal camouflage
- **present** a news broadcast about an amazing animal
- **write** a leaflet about an animal rescue centre
- **read** a poem about pets.

Getting started

Why should we look after animals and their habitat?

a What types of animals can you see in each photo?
b Which photo shows an animal helping someone?
c What challenges do many animals face?
d Are they similar to us in any way?
   What's special about them?

Watch this!

› 9.1 Animal habitats

We are going to...

- **talk and find out about animal habitats.**

horned viper

1 **Vocabulary: Where do you think these animals live? Match them with their habitat.**

a forest

b Antarctic

c freshwater

d mountain

e ocean

f desert

stick insect

 2 **Listen and check your answers.**

3 **Talk: What's in a name? Look closely at the names and study the photo of the animals in Activity 1. Why do you think they have these names? Share opinions with your partner.**

elephant seal

Language focus – Compound nouns

A compound noun is a noun that can be made up of two or more words.

1 noun + noun (one word) **butterfly**

2 noun + noun (two words) **stick insect**

3 adjective + noun **grizzly bear**

clownfish

4 **Use of English: What compound noun patterns can you find in Activity 1?**

African dwarf frog

golden eagle

5 **Listen again and take notes.**
Can you think of more animals that live in these habitats?

	Type of animal	Name of animal	Habitat	Eats
1	Reptile			Lizards and birds
2		Stick insect		Small bugs

6 Read: **What problems is the clownfish facing? Circle the dangers in the text.**

Losing Nemo

The famous clownfish from the film *Finding Nemo* is in danger. The main problems are pollution of the oceans and the change in sea temperatures. Warmer water affects all kinds of habitats especially coral reefs, which are the clownfish's natural habitat. The clown fish lives in the anemones, which are a protective home from other fish that want to eat it. So if the reefs die, the clownfish will have nowhere to live. How can we help protect its habitat?

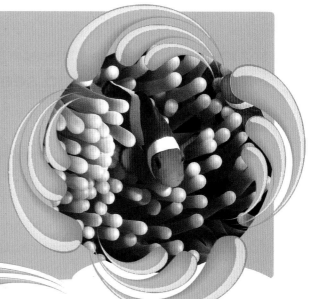

7 Use of English: **Find three more preposition + noun examples in Activity 6.**

8 **Use modal verbs to talk about how we can help sea animals in their habitat.**

> We mustn't throw plastic into the sea.

Language focus

Prepositions + noun

We often use certain prepositions before nouns to describe them.

The famous clownfish is **in danger**.

> 9.2 Animal camouflage

We are going to...

- read a text and learn about animal camouflage.

1 **Read and listen:** How do animals adapt to their environment?
How do they protect themselves? Read and listen to check your ideas.

Animal hide and seek

Most animals need to be very clever in order to survive in the animal kingdom. One of their most amazing skills is called **camouflage** – their bodies copy the colour of their environment to hide from their **predator** or to help them hunt for their **prey**.

The chameleon can't move very quickly, so camouflage is important to its survival. It can change its colour to copy all kinds of backgrounds. This way it can protect its territory and itself from predators.

The pygmy seahorse is a tiny animal that is between 1.4 and 2.7 cm long. They live in coral reefs and suck their prey through their tube-like mouth. Their camouflage is so good that it's very difficult to see them in their **habitats**.

The cuttlefish with its green blood and three hearts is also excellent at camouflage. It can change colour in seconds, but it can also change its body shape to look like something else if a hungry predator comes along! If it is chased by a predator, it shoots ink into the sea. This makes the water cloudy, so it can escape more easily.

Key words: Animal life

camouflage: when animals change colour to adapt to the colours around them
predator: an animal that hunts and kills other animals
prey: an animal that is hunted and killed for food by another animal
habitat: where animals live

2 **Read the text again and find the following:**

    a   Two things animals do in order to survive.

    b   What the pygmy seahorse does to its prey.

    c   Two strange characteristics of the cuttlefish.

    d   Another way in which the cuttlefish can camouflage itself.

3 **Use of English:** Look at the Use of English box and match the animal it describes in the text. Can you find more examples of the use of *it* or *its* in the text?

4 **Talk:** Play a game. Guess the animal. With a partner take turns to describe and guess an animal.

> **Use of English – it/its**
>
> We use **it** instead of the name of the place, object or animal so that we don't repeat the name. We use **its** if something belongs to the animal.
>
> **It** shoots ink into the sea. It can change **its** colour to copy…

Does it live in the (forest)?

Does it eat _____ (plants)?

5 **Word study:** Look at the animals below and use the words in the box to describe how these characteristics help them. Use *it/its* when you can.

big ears	a long tail	scales	**a hump**	a long neck	**stripes**

> 9.3 Animals in the media

We are going to...

- present a news broadcast/report about amazing animals.

1 **Read** the headlines. How do you think these animals saved someone's life?

A

B

C

 2 **Listen** and match each description to an animal in Activity 1.

 3 **Listen** again. Are these sentences true or false?

    a   The dolphins hit the water with their fins. _____

    b   The dog couldn't wake up its owner. _____

    c   The dog saved the lives of the people in the house and their other pets. _____

    d   The parrot was eating Hanna's breakfast. _____

    e   The mother ran to save Hanna when she heard the parrot. _____

Use of English – Gerund and infinitives

He **decided to go** for a swim.
The parrot **enjoyed eating** breakfast with Hanna.

4 **Use of English: Complete the sentences from the news reports using a gerund or the infinitive.**

   a The dolphins kept _____ (swim) with them.
   b They plan _____ (have) a special party for Molly.
   c Hanna's mother left the room to finish _____ (prepare) her bag.
   d She stopped _____ (pack) and ran back into the room.

5 **Talk: What do you think of these amazing animals? Has an animal ever helped you?**

6 **Pronunciation: Listen to the words with short and long vowel sounds. Write them in the correct column. Can you add two more words to each column?**

Short sound	Long sound
fins	sea

Speaking tip

Language for news reports

Hello and welcome to...
Today we are talking about...
Let's turn to a story about...
And finally, a story about...
Well, thank you everyone for...

7 **Present a live news report in class.**

   - In pairs, research a local or national news story online.
   - Take notes about what happened and where.
   - Use some of the useful phrases in the Speaking tip for your report.
   - Take turns to present your live report.
   - Record your news stories (optional).

9.4 Animal Rescue

We are going to...

- write a leaflet for an animal rescue centre.

1 **Talk:** Have you ever visited a farm, a safari park or an animal rescue centre? Was it a school or a family trip? What animals did you see? What did you do?

2 **Read:** What does this animal rescue centre do? Read this leaflet to find out.

general information

imperatives

SOS Primates!

We are a primate rescue centre. We give a new home to primates that have lost theirs or have been abandoned and can't return to their natural habitat.

At our centre we have chimpanzees, gorillas, macaques and our oldest and most famous resident Ollie the Orangutan!

Come along and enjoy watching the primates play in their spacious natural enclosure.

Help during **feeding time**, which is always great fun, and don't miss our **guided tour** with our top primatologist!

Find out about the different species we have and their individual stories. It will be a day to remember!

Opening times

Tues–Sun 10 a.m. – 6 p.m.

Closed Mondays.

(except bank holidays during school term time)

Prices:

Adults: £8

Pensioners: £6.50

Children: (2–14 yrs) £6

Under 2 yrs: Free Admission

interesting activities

3 **Read the text again and find this information.**

a four types of primates
b three activities you can do there
c someone who knows a lot about primates
d a well-known primate at the centre
e the price under 2s need to pay

4 Write: **Design and write a leaflet for an animal farm or rescue centre.**

Step 1: Ideas (collaboration)	• Research information online about a rescue centre or farm and the animals that live there. • Make a list of the activities people can do there. • Find photos to put in your leaflet.
Step 2: Planning your leaflet	Decide what information to put onto your leaflet. Don't forget to include opening times and prices.
Step 3: Writing	Write your leaflet using the example in Activity 2 to help you.

5 **Now you have finished your leaflet, check that you have included everything on the checklist.**

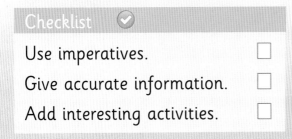

Checklist ✓

Use imperatives. ☐
Give accurate information. ☐
Add interesting activities. ☐

〉 9.5 Mum won't let me keep a rabbit

1　Talk: Have you ever asked for a pet that you couldn't have?
How did you feel? Why couldn't you have it?

 2　Read and **listen** to the poem.
Find the animals from the poem in the pictures.

Mum won't let me keep a rabbit

Mum won't let me keep a rabbit,
She won't let me keep a bat,
She won't let me keep a porcupine
Or a water-rat.

I can't keep pigeons
And I can't keep snails,
I can't keep kangaroos
Or wallabies with nails.

She won't let me keep a rattlesnake
Or a viper in the house,
She won't let me keep a mamba
Or its meal, a mouse.

She won't let me keep a wombat
And it isn't very clear,
Why I can't keep iguanas,
jelly fish or deer.

I can't keep a cockroach
or a bumblebee,
I can't keep an earwig
A maggot or a flea.

I can't keep a wildebeest
And it's just my luck
I can't keep a mallard,
A dabchick or a duck.

She won't let me keep piranhas,
Toads or even frogs,
She won't let me keep an octopus
Or muddy water-hogs.

So out in the garden I keep a pet ant
And up in the attic ! TNAHPELE TERCES A

Brian Patten

3   **What animal does the poet keep in the attic? Reorder the letters to find out.**

4 Pronunciation: **Find words in the poem that rhyme with these animals. Then listen and check.**

a bat   b snails   c deer

d bumblebee   e duck   f water-hogs

5 Word study: **Put the animals from the poem into groups. Use your dictionary to check the meaning of the words you don't know.**

Mammals	Insects	Birds	Amphibians	Reptiles	Sea animals/fish
	Flea				

6 Write **three sentences about the animals from the poem you'd like to keep and three about those you wouldn't like to keep.**

I'd like to keep a...   I wouldn't like to keep a...

7 Write **a verse about the animals you are sure you can't keep in your house. Try to make the words in line two and line four rhyme.**

I can't keep a _____

And I can't keep a _____ (rhyming word)

I can't keep a _____

Or a _____ with _____ (rhyming word)

8 **Find out information about one of the animals in the poem you hadn't heard of before. Write a paragraph about it and find a picture.**

Type of animal: Rabbit

Behaviour: sleeps most of the day

Diet: grass, herbs, flowers

Habitat: fields

Characteristics: small, brown, white or black fur, long ears, big feet, good sense of smell

9 **Read and listen** to these animal alliterations
Match each one to the correct illustration.
What do you notice about the words?

a

b

1   Larry the lucky lion laughed loudly as he leaped over
Lucy the lazy lizard while she lovingly licked a lemon lollipop.
2   Charlie the cheerful cheetah chose to chew cheese and
cherries as he chomped his chops.

10 Circle the correct definition for alliteration.

a   The words all rhyme.

b   The main words all start with the same sound.

11 Look at the guide below and complete the table.
You don't have to think of a word for every column.

Name	Size/shape	Colour	Animal	Action verb	Adverb/noun
Sid	(the) small	silver	_____	slithers	slowly
Pete	_____	(the) purple	_____	paints pictures	_____

12 Write your own animal alliteration. Use the guide to help you.
Draw a picture to illustrate your alliteration.

13 Values: Respecting and caring for animals.
Discuss the questions in groups.

a   How can we help to protect animal habitats?
b   Why is it important to look after animals and pets in our care?
c   What do animal rescue centres do and why?
d   If you have a pet, explain how you care for it.

> 9.6 Project challenge

Project A: A nature study

1   What are the animal habitats below? Is there a habitat in or around your school like one of these? What animals do you think you could find there?

2   Choose a habitat that interests you the most and study it over a number of days. Take notes on:

- The conditions of the habitat (*dry, humid...*)
- The insects and animals that live there.
- Find out what they eat (prey) and what eats them (predator).
- Choose one of the insects or animals and draw a picture of it.
- Label the parts of its body.

3   Present your findings to the class.

Project B: Make a 'Save the Primate' poster

1 Look at the primates. Which problem do you think they all share?

gorillas

macaques

orangutans

2 In groups, choose one of the primates you would like to make a poster about and divide up the tasks below.

- Take notes about the primate's habitat, size, diet and characteristics.
- Investigate online to find out why this species is in danger.
  Write notes **under these headings**.

Problem   **Reason**   **Action**

3 Make your poster.

- Write a title for your poster 'SAVE THE... (name of primate)'.
- Draw a picture of your primate. Label its characteristics.
- Use your notes to write a short paragraph about why it's in danger, the reason, and action that needs to be taken.

4 Display your poster in class and present your group findings.

What did you like most about this project? What's the most important thing you've learned from it?

> 9.7 What do you know now?

What lessons can we learn from the animal kingdom?

1 Write the name of two animals that live in each habitat.

forest   Antarctic   grassland   mountain

freshwater   ocean   desert

2 Why is the clownfish in danger?

3 Write five examples of animal compound nouns.

4 What do we need to do to protect animal habitats? Write sentences using:

have to   must

should   need to

5 Write a sentence or sentences about an animal using *it* and *its*.

6 How have animals saved people's lives?

7 Give an example of how an animal adapts to its environment.

Look what I can do

Write or show examples in your notebook.

I can talk about animal habitats.

I can use modal verbs to talk about how we can protect a sea animal's habitat.

I can understand a text about animal camouflage.

I can present a news broadcast about an amazing animal.

I can write a leaflet about an animal rescue centre.

I can read and understand a poem about pets.

Check your progress 3

1 **Read the riddles and guess the words.**

a I'm a form of Ancient Egyptian writing.

b I'm at the bottom of the rainforest.

c You breathe me in.

d I am a very watery habitat.

e Ancient Romans like to wear me on their feet.

f I'm a poisonous little amphibian with red eyes.

g I'm an ancient Egyptian invention that you write on.

h I'm an orange and white fish which lives in the coral reefs.

i I'm a dry habitat and home to the horned viper.

2 **Write the words in these categories. Add two more words to each one.**

Ancient civilisations	Rainforests	Animal kingdom
hieroglyphics		

3 **Choose two words from Units 7–9. Write two riddles of your own for your partner to guess.**

4 **Play the 10 questions game and follow the instructions.**

• In small groups, each person take turns to think of a word.

• The rest of the group asks yes / no questions to find out what the word is.

• Remember you can only ask a maximum of 10 questions.

Is it an animal?

Does it live in the forest?

No, it isn't.

Yes, it does.

5 **Circle the correct answers.**

a People believe **of / that** the sphinx guarded the Pharoah's tomb.

b They found the treasure **at / on** 10th April 1945 **at / on** the bottom of the sea.

c The people **has / have** lived in the village **since / for** centuries.

d The rubber tree produces **extremely / a little** large amounts of latex.

e A monkey uses **it's / its** long tail to swing from tree to tree.

f He enjoys **to swim / swimming** in the sea in the summer.

g She **has / have** decided **visiting / to visit** the Pyramids this summer.

h A sloth has got **long, sharp / sharp, long** claws.

6 **In small groups write six quiz questions about ancient civilisations, rainforests and animals and their habitats. Give them to another group to answer. Look back through the units to find the answers.**

What percentage of the world's plants and animals live in the rainforest?

7 **Play 'Simon Says'. Work in pairs and follow the instructions.**

- **Student A:** Choose one of the actions below and give instructions to your partner. Say 'Simon Says...' for some of your instructions.
- **Student B:** Do as Student A tells you when he/she says 'Simon Says...' When your partner gives you an instruction but doesn't say Simon Says, **don't** do the activity.

mix   cut   crush   roll   catch   pick

Simon Says, cut a carrot!

Mix some eggs and flour!